Living Latin

Rubicon

Series editor
Thomas Harrison

This new series seeks to challenge and refresh the study of antiquity: to re-examine central texts and questions, to disrupt stale orthodoxies, to test and problematize the nature and limits of our disciplines, to champion new approaches and to respond to the latest developments in research and in our contemporary world. Rubicon breaks through barriers – to open up the history, literature and culture of the ancient world.

Titles in the series
What Is a Jewish Classicist?: Essays on the Personal Voice and Disciplinary Politics by Simon Goldhill

Living Latin

Everyday Language and Popular Culture

Charlie Kerrigan

BLOOMSBURY ACADEMIC
LONDON • NEW YORK • OXFORD • NEW DELHI • SYDNEY

BLOOMSBURY ACADEMIC
Bloomsbury Publishing Plc
50 Bedford Square, London, WC1B 3DP, UK
1385 Broadway, New York, NY 10018, USA
29 Earlsfort Terrace, Dublin 2, Ireland

BLOOMSBURY, BLOOMSBURY ACADEMIC and the Diana logo are trademarks of Bloomsbury Publishing Plc

First published in Great Britain 2024

Cover design: Terry Woodley

A catalogue record for this book is available from the British Library.

A catalog record for this book is available from the Library of Congress.

ISBN: HB: 978-1-3503-7702-8
PB: 978-1-3503-7703-5
ePDF: 978-1-3503-7704-2
eBook: 978-1-3503-7705-9

Series: Rubicon

Typeset by RefineCatch Limited, Bungay, Suffolk

To find out more about our authors and books visit www.bloomsbury.com and sign up for our newsletters.

Contents

Illustrations

Preface

This essay on the history of Latin is meant for students and teachers, as well as anyone curious about the language. I've done my best to write clearly, and to gather together the work of scholars which a general audience might find interesting and useful. There are no footnotes; instead, you'll find a list of the works I've used – alongside material you can explore further in your own time – at the end. My hope is that you'll discover a language a little different to the one you might have imagined.

This book comes from a blog written over the last number of years called *Confabulations*, its title taken from the art historian John Berger (1926–2017). *Confabulations* is part of the Living Latin project at Trinity College, Dublin, where I and a team of colleagues have been trying to make a subject with a reputation for difficulty and exclusivity more welcoming and inclusive, particularly for beginners. The book, no less than the blog, is a series of personal takes, inspired by writers and artists from Ireland and around the world. Its main inspiration on the Latin side has been the work of J. N. Adams (1943–2021), who did so much to change and deepen our understanding of Latin and its history. In a blog post published in 2020, Jim outlined in a few paragraphs the case for the diversity of Latin, and it's that thread that I've been following here. My other inspiration has been Howard Zinn's *A People's History of the United States*. Zinn (1922–2010) was a war veteran and political activist as well as a historian, who believed that history is lived and made by ordinary people just as much as it is by politicians, generals, and statesmen. To write history only in terms of the latter is to give them and their actions undue privilege, and to ignore the ways in which genuinely progressive politics can come from the bottom up, rather than the top down.

Chapter 1 looks at everyday language and the evidence for the lives of ordinary people, particularly working people, in the history of Latin; I've tried to keep in mind here the words of the American poet Adrienne Rich (1929–2012), who wrote that 'Writing and teaching are kinds of work, and the relative creative freedom of the writer or teacher depends on the conditions of human labour overall and everywhere.' Chapter 2 is a tour through a few famous texts from ancient Rome and their history in popular culture, as well as their relevance to modern times: the lesson here is that art and culture are common human things, which live and flourish independently of wealthy institutions and official recognition. In Chapter 3 I cover Latin's journey to Romance, tracing its high and low branches from the end of the Roman empire to the twenty-first century, and coming round full circle to a language of ordinary people and everyday life.

To avoid confusion, this is not a book about spoken Latin in modern society, sometimes referred to as 'Living Latin', or its use in education ('the active method'). I mean instead to evoke the diverse world of communication as it exists in truly living languages, as well as the ways in which stories from any culture take on lives of their own. My sense is that by focusing on these two things – linguistic diversity and creative reimagining – it becomes much harder to tell the story of Latin in narrow or elitist ways. You'll find the abbreviations BCE (Before the Common Era) and CE (Common Era) throughout: these are secular versions of the traditional BC and AD of the Gregorian calendar.

A big thank you to everyone who has supported this work over the last few years. To Anna Chahoud, first and foremost, who started the Living Latin project and who has been an unfailing support in my work on the blog and in my teaching to date; to my colleagues in the Department of Classics at TCD for their encouragement and comradery at every stage, to Trish Stapleton and Pat Carty in the School of Histories and Humanities, and to Kevin, Paul, and Frank at the Living Latin project. For publishing this book and for help in editing and production, sincere thanks to Thomas Harrison, series editor, alongside Alice Wright, Lily Mac Mahon, and Zoë Osman at Bloomsbury, and for further support and encouragement to Jon Davies, Cosetta Cadau, Helen McVeigh, and Giacomo Fedeli. I am indebted to the work of the scholars quoted below, and any remaining errors are my own. For help in practical matters thanks to the Library and Arts Building staff at Trinity. Thanks lastly to my family and friends: to my parents, Paul and Marie, and my siblings, Olivia and Jack; to Billy, Ciarán, Rob, Simon, Eleanor, Glenn, Venina, and Justin; to David and Malcolm, Róisín and Martin, Trish and Jim, Iseult and James, Mnemo and Alastair, Lisa and Simon; to Johnny, Mary, and Lauren. I'd like to dedicate this book to the TCD extramural students, whose company on Wednesday evenings over a number of years now has been a joy, and whose common-sense enthusiasm for Latin has led the way.

C.K.
Dublin, May 2023

1

The Latin of Ordinary People

Latin is many things, but for those who encounter it in formal education, it is the language of ancient Rome and the ancient Romans, recorded in a series of texts that have been interpreted, praised, and read for centuries. A language of senators and consuls, proud generals and tyrannical emperors, famous poets and eloquent politicians. In short, a language of powerful men and powerful institutions. This holds true after the Roman empire, too, when Latin became the language of one branch of Christianity, its cardinals, popes, and philosophers, and the medieval universities of Europe. It has been used ever since ancient times to teach the children of powerful families, to prepare them for important and high-powered careers, with boys (so I suspect) usually outnumbering girls. It has often been the concern of the most privileged sections of society, and has been shaped to reflect their interests and their aspirations. The daily lives of ancient Romans have always been interesting to students of the language, but here too the picture is narrower than it could be. Latin is most often a language of villas and banquets, of temples and slave-owning noble families, of cruel gladiatorial displays and triumphal parades through the city of Rome. This image of ancient Rome has also shaped ideas about Latin in popular culture. You can see it, for instance, in Hollywood movies from the 1960s to the present day, and in the novels about life in the ancient city.

Latin and its cousin, ancient Greek, have always provided readers with strange and fantastic stories which speak to alternative ways of being and thinking, stories that disrupt simplistic ideas about society and sexuality. Latin is a language of gods and goddesses, myths and legends, which still inspires today. Even in this context, however, it is a language of the extraordinary, of high literature and high politics. This says something about what we look for in the past: heroic deeds and old-time heroes, 'A tune beyond us, yet ourselves' as the American poet Wallace Stevens put it. The Latin classics deserve consideration in their own right, and we'll get to them in Chapter 2. Here I simply want to point out that focus on these classics has limited what the Latin language is taken to be. In textbooks for learning Latin, despite a certain attention to the details of daily life, the vocabulary still tends to feature a lot of swords, soldiers, and slave-owning, while original texts for translation still tend to be drawn from a small pool of works, the most famous part of Latin literature, which date from between 200 BCE and 200 CE. This is partly a bias built up over many generations, and reflects a belief, not necessarily misplaced, in the value of such classics. It is partly a pragmatic move to prepare students to read texts which at a more advanced level are disproportionately focused on war and affairs of state. But to focus on this kind of material is a choice, and things could be done differently.

Take the phrase *veni, vidi, vici*, or 'I came, I saw, I conquered'. It's one of the most famous pieces of Latin that there is, and it was said by perhaps the most famous Roman of all: Julius Caesar, the general who conquered Gaul, reformed the calendar, inspired Shakespeare, and whose name became quite literally synonymous with power (as in

Kaiser, Tsar, Cesare). The phrase was put on a sign and carried in one of Caesar's triumphs (or victory parades) through the streets of Rome in 46 BCE, boasting about the speed of a particular military victory. It can tell us something about the history of Latin.

The phrase displays a fondness for wordplay that reflects elite Rome education and its concern with public speaking. Three short words, each of two syllables, and each beginning and ending with the same sound. The idea of grouping things in three is something familiar in English ('game, set, and match') and it makes the phrase memorable. What we have, in other words, is a brilliant piece of PR, one which is often reused and reworked in modern advertising. Roman triumphs were festive but brutal affairs, at which prisoners were sometimes paraded through the streets of the city in chains; Caesar's slogan reminds me of George W. Bush on the aircraft carrier with his giant 'Mission Accomplished' banner. *Veni, vidi, vici,* furthermore, represents the kind of Latin that has always been centre stage, the kind that has been prized and valued by those involved in the teaching and learning of the language. Caesar represents the multi-talented man of action which traditional Roman history is full of: a commanding general, public-speaker, author, and politician. He is the author of third-person accounts of his military campaigning in Roman Gaul (modern France) and in a Roman civil war. He is exactly the kind of author still used to accustom elementary Latin students to the classical language, those texts dating from between 200 BCE and 200 CE. And yet his military actions in France amount to what many would today call a series of war crimes. The important thing is not to cancel Caesar, but to tell the truth about him (I paraphrase Howard Zinn on Columbus), and, as teachers, to think carefully about what and how we teach.

So when the students are learning about the Romans, I ask them: which Romans do you mean? It seems obvious to me that the different kinds of people I encounter today existed back in ancient times, it's just that the generals and politicians and writers take up most of the space. We know about the triumphal parades, but what about the anti-war protests? We know about the lavish banquets, but what about the simple meals of bread, barley, and garden vegetables on which most people lived? What evidence is there for the lives of ordinary people? Quite a bit, as it turns out, and some of it will be the subject of this chapter. But before we leave Caesar it's important to remember that the classics are always there to be reimagined, the property of no one. He and his phrase have been stripped for parts in many later contexts. He's there in Seán Clárach Mac Domhnaill's lament for Bonnie Prince Charlie and the Jacobite cause, *Bímse buan ar buairt gach ló* ('My Heart is Sore with Sorrow Deep'), 'Caesar' now the hope of an oppressed majority in eighteenth-century Ireland:

> He is my hero, fair and fleet,
> He is my Caesar, fair and fleet,
> I get no rest, I cannot sleep,
> Since he crossed the ocean, fair and fleet.

Caesar's three-word phrase has also entered the English language, often used without any reference to ancient Rome. It's there in a song from the 1930s, *These Foolish Things (Remind Me of You)*, with lyrics by Eric Maschwitz and music by Jack Strachey, and first recorded by the Grenadian singer and entertainer Leslie 'Hutch' Hutchinson (1900–69) in London in 1935. The bridge of the song features our phrase, but it's been reworked, and the point of view has been changed. Soon after it first appeared, Billie Holiday (1915–59) recorded her version of the song in New York, backed by Teddy Wilson and his orchestra. A twenty-one-year-old Holiday sets the lyric alight with the way she makes a soft wail out of the first 'me', with the knowing emphasis she puts on 'that' in the second line (if you search for the song online and listen, you'll see what I mean). All the ambivalence of conquest, now romantic rather than military, is suggested. The racism and patriarchy of the society in which Holiday grew up meant that formal educational access to Latin (indeed, much formal education at all) was not available to her. Yet she makes the phrase completely her own.

*

Latin was a language in which ordinary people lived their lives for many centuries, used for all the things language is still used for. To love and hate, to argue and wound, to chat and gossip. The problem is that language is first and foremost something spoken, not written, and, as J. N. Adams noted, there are no sound recordings of native speakers of Latin, no time machines in which we can go back to hear them talking. Ancient Latin texts represent the tip of a very large iceberg, with a great mass of language hidden beneath the surface. To try and imagine what spoken Latin was like, I think about the living language that I know best: the English spoken in Ireland in the first part of the twenty-first century. This language exists alongside many other languages, both verbal and non-verbal; it is continually being marked by different influences and the different peoples who come to the island. This has given it its own unique and varied soundscape, from Cork to Derry and from Dublin to Galway. English in Ireland is a colonial language, as Latin was in many places, and it is full of American sounds and words because of the influence of the United States in modern times. Yet it has been shot through with Irish structures, whenever someone says, 'I'm after losing my keys', 'You've the work done', or 'Don't be saying that', and if you travel around you can see placenames so awkwardly translated into English that they practically remain in the original. Irish English is full of words which have particular meanings in Ireland and nowhere else. It is an immensely rich and varied language.

Imagine, then, that you could step into a time machine and journey two thousand years into the future; suppose that humanity has been able to survive, and a historian is looking into the language spoken in Ireland in the 2020s CE. It's not clear how much material she would have to go on, how much our online world will be preserved for the historians of the future. She might assume that people in Ireland said 'Hello', 'goodbye', 'please' and 'thank you', based on a selection of written sources, which are by their nature conservative, and perhaps not even from Ireland. The *Oxford English Dictionary* would only help her so much, though if she had access to messaging and internet speak that might be considerably more useful. She might, in any case, end up with quite an inaccurate picture, because people in Ireland when they speak English rarely say, simply: hello, goodbye, please, and thank you. They instead say things like *hi* and *howiye*, *g'wan* and *cheers* and *thanks a mil*; they say *sound* and *grand* and *no bother*, *go raibh míle* (thanks), *slán* (goodbye), and *aon scéal?* (any news?). They speak with different accents and tones and registers depending on who they're talking to, each time they talk. The richness of the living language might escape her notice.

It's the same for Latin. We know that the language was full of social and regional variation, that it had different sounds in different places and that people spoke differently in different situations. It's just that the evidence for such variation is scarce. Everything that survives, survives in writing, and writing is inherently conservative. None of us write exactly as we speak, and most languages allow for a degree of slippage between spoken and written forms: think of silent letters, and the many English words that can sound the same despite being spelled differently. Or how you're talking, next time you're talking quickly to a close friend. Yet evidence for variation in Latin does exist, and we have enough of it to be able to prove that there was no one way in which people spoke. Some of this evidence has been known about for centuries – ever since the days of ancient Rome – while a lot of it has been discovered very recently, only in the last fifty years, even within the last ten. This new evidence is exciting because it is changing the history of Latin by showing us more diversity than ever before. It comes from all over the Roman world: on papyri from Egypt, bits of pottery from Libya and southern France, lead tablets from southern England, and frail letters of ink and birchwood from an army camp near Hadrian's Wall. The history of Latin is newer than it has ever been.

There is an old idea of 'vulgar' Latin, 'vulgar' meaning 'of the people', a spoken language that ran parallel to the high ('classical') language of the Roman elite and their literature, which over time turned into the modern Romance languages. This idea has a grain of truth to it, but it has been substantially revised by modern scholarship. There are words which appear in earlier Latin texts which are not found in the high classical period (say between 80 BCE and 120 CE) but which then reappear in the Romance languages. Like the verb *fabulari*, to chat, which appears in the comedies of Plautus and Terence (*c.* 200–160 BCE), is absent in later literature, but then reappears in Spanish (*hablar*) and Portuguese (*falar*) as the verb 'to speak'. This is what scholars refer to as 'submerged' Latin, suggesting that the word (and others like it) must have had a currency in everyday language if it survives in Romance. The point, however, is not that there were two Latins – one for the emperors and poets and another for the common people – but that any language user can speak or write more formally or more informally depending on the context. There is a fragment of a letter from Augustus, the first Roman emperor, in which he writes of 'eating two mouthfuls' in words that are rarely found in the classical language, but which anticipate modern Italian. The historian Livy, one of the authors who, alongside Cicero, has been held up as a model of classical style, constantly breaks a rule found in every Latin textbook, relating to the use of a particular preposition. At the same time, many stone inscriptions – not all of them elite sources – are written in elegant and literary verse forms.

In the tradition of linguistics represented by Noam Chomsky and many others, language is not just the sensory-motor act of speaking, but something which structures human consciousness, a 'species property' which humans share with little intrinsic variation. It is by its nature a creative and independent faculty, which operates free from external control and is subject to the individual's wishes: no one can quite tell what any of us is going to say next. In other words, before we get to writing, let alone to literature, language is already something creative and imaginative. Think of all the people who spoke Latin but never wrote it down, who may not have been able to read and write, yet whose language was as rich as anyone else's. Or the magic of storytelling and song culture in many parts of the world, which thrives in oral rather than written form. Once you understand this diversity, it becomes much harder to imagine just one kind of Latin. The generals, emperors, and poets recede from view a little, and you can fill up your idea of Latin with the different kinds of people, and the different kinds of situations, that you still encounter today. Latin was once a language of first dates and funerals, arguments and gossip, birthday parties, pub conversations, and baby talk. Like any language, it often failed, and was used by people to be horrible to each other, 'busy doing inhumanly human things'. While there are no sound recordings or time machines, we have enough evidence to appreciate its diversity.

My focus here comes from a tradition which believes that history-writing is a question, not just of facts, but of emphasis: which stories are told, and for what reasons. Despite much ongoing work to redress the balance, my sense is that Latin studies still tend to focus disproportionately on ruling classes, their interests and affairs. To give them such a privileged position is understandable, and they are part of the human story like any other group. The story of language is that everyone is, in some sense, an ordinary person, yet this shouldn't blind us to the ways in which networks of power, wealth, and privilege sustain themselves across multiple generations to real and damaging effect. Often those ruling classes – Roman, Christian, or both – presided over systems of government which were deeply unfair (being imperial, militaristic, patriarchal, and autocratic) and have inspired similar systems of government ever since. The challenge for the historian, by contrast, for me can be summed up in these lines by Arundhati Roy, from her essay 'The End of Imagination':

> To never get used to the unspeakable violence and the vulgar disparity of life around you. To seek joy in the saddest places. To pursue beauty to its lair. To never simplify what is complicated or complicate what is simple. To respect strength, never power. Above all, to watch. To try and understand. To never look away. And never, never to forget.

The lives and struggles of ordinary people are no less rich and no less worthy of study, full of lessons in how we might live sustainably and justly in the twenty-first century, as well as full of failure and frustration. You do not need to romanticise them in some simplistic or naïve way in order to learn something.

So while I mean 'the Latin of ordinary people' as inclusively as possible, this chapter is an attempt to take the spotlight off the usual suspects and put it onto some lesser known evidence, particularly evidence for the lives of working people. What will emerge, I hope, is a more diverse and colourful history of Latin. So much of the present moment can be understood in terms of people's everyday concerns: for equitable distribution of wealth, for a liveable planet, for sanctuary for those fleeing war and persecution, for an end to murderous structures of institutional racism and violence. In a real and sobering way, the human future will be defined by humans' ability to enact change globally and collectively, whatever the plans of some to escape to a private safe-house, or to Mars.

*

Latin began life as the language of one, very small, part of the Italian peninsula, in and around what is now the city of Rome. It existed alongside many other languages throughout the peninsula and its neighbouring islands, long before anyone had ever heard of the Roman empire: languages like Etruscan, Ligurian, and Venetic to the north; Greek, Oscan, and Messapic to the south. The earliest datable pieces of Latin come from the seventh century BCE – some 2,600 years ago – and include a golden brooch found in the nineteenth century near the town of Palestrina (see Figure 1 at the end of this chapter). It is a luxury artefact, buried in a grave, but it is also the work of an artisan, a skilled craftsperson, who, if you believe the brooch to be authentic (and there have been debates about this ever since it was discovered) has signed his creation. The text is written right to left, in the Etruscan manner, and it says:

> Manios made me for Numasios

There are perhaps seventeen inscriptions in total which can be dated to the seventh and sixth centuries BCE, most of our evidence for the language comes later. This evidence showcases the growth of Roman power in the peninsula, certainly, and includes the proud and boastful inscriptions of well-to-do citizens, conquering generals, and the magistrates of the Roman republic. But it also gives us glimpses into the lives of labourers, shopkeepers, and craftspeople busy about their work.

Sometime around 100 BCE, two women were working on a rooftop in a settlement in central Italy, in a place known today as

Pietrabbondante. We know these women's names, that they were unfree labourers, that they spoke different languages, and that they were literate. How do we know? Because a tile survives with their footprints and signatures on it, discovered in 1975. Their names were Detfri and Amica. Detfri has signed in Oscan, the central Italian language still spoken up until at least the end of the first century BCE, while Amica ('Friend') has signed in Latin; both include the Oscan form of their owner's name:

> Detfri of Herens Sattis signed with a footprint
> Amica of Herens signed when we were laying out the tile

As Katherine McDonald notes, we have perhaps ten minutes in the lives of these women. We know so little about them, have more questions than answers, yet a tiny part of their personalities and their situation is preserved for us. The tile highlights the diversity of ancient Italy, its different languages, its different people: the survival of Oscan in an increasingly Latin world, as well as the bilingualism of workers in an economy based on unfree labour. Language acquisition is for many people a necessity rather than a luxury, one achieved with little ceremony. The tile helps us towards what scholars today would call an *intersectional* understanding, recognising those groups – like unfree women – who are always less seen, more ignored, than more privileged groups in society, then and now.

The first century BCE is an important one in the story of Italy. Ten years or so after Detfri and Amica signed their tile, Rome's Italian allies went to war against the Roman state, by now the major political player in the peninsula, in a revolt known as The Social War (*socius* in Latin = 'ally'). The rebels set up a capital which they called *Italica* near modern Corfinio in central Italy; they minted their own coins – which still survive today – on which the bull of Italy has the Roman she-wolf by the neck. Their motivations are not entirely clearly to us, but we know enough to know that they were fighting for a greater degree of equality in an increasingly Roman world. The rebellion was put down by the Roman army, led by its consuls (its military leaders), and a post-war settlement was enacted which led to a massive expansion of Roman citizenship within Italy. Not for the last time, colonisation and attempted centralisation by an increasingly powerful state brought Latin in its wake, as other regional languages began to be put under pressure by its spread. The end of the first century BCE is the time when the Roman republic – nominally a state governed 'by the Senate and People of Rome' (SPQR), but really a militaristic oligarchy – collapses after a series of bitter civil wars, to give way to a new system of government under the leadership of Octavian, the first Roman emperor (though remember that Rome was an empire long before it was called so). This is what most people mean when they talk about Roman history. Yet despite Octavian's boast that 'all Italy' had rowed in behind him in his defeat of Mark Antony and Cleopatra in 31 BCE, the peninsula was never a completely Roman place. Its linguistic and ethnic diversity has never gone away, and lives on today in the diversity of the modern Italian state.

Octavian was awarded the name 'Augustus' – 'revered one' – by the Senate in 27 BCE, and reigned until his death in 14 CE. By this period Ravenna on the north-eastern coast of Italy was an important port and naval centre for the Roman state, a state kept going by its workers and soldiers and farmers, both free and unfree, most of them unknown to history. It is to this period that we can date a funeral monument to a Ravenna shipbuilder, his wife, and two of his freedmen, or ex-slaves (see Figure 2 at the end of this chapter). The man was a Roman citizen, but he appears to have had a Celtic name, concealing the roots of the Irish words *long* ('ship') and *dían* ('fast'). The stone monument features two pairs of carved likenesses, one above the other, above a further scene of a man at work. The top pair are Longidienus and his wife,

Longidiena, herself a freedwoman, whose face on the monument has been badly damaged:

> Publius Longidienus, son of Publius, of the tribe of Camilia, shipbuilder, established [this monument] while he was alive also for Longidiena Stacte, freedwoman of Publius.

Below them are the two companions, with the accompanying inscription:

> Publius Longidienus Rufio, freedman of Publius, and Publius Longidienus Piladespotus, freedman of Publius, paid the cost [of the monument] to their *patronus*.

As with the roof-tile, there is much that we would like to know, especially about the relationship and power dynamic between these four people, three of them former slaves of the fourth. The three freedpeople have each taken their name from their former master, while Rufio and Piladespotus have paid for the monument.

The case is to be left open, though as John Clarke notes, in his book *Art in the Lives of Ordinary Romans*, the monument could well represent a *familia* or household based on mutual respect and affection. At the same time, it would be wrong to celebrate Longidienus as a virtuous and happy patriarch, and we simply can't tell precisely what relationships existed behind the monument's warm and generous façade. What is clearer is that the commissioners of the piece wanted to emphasise the pride that Longidienus took in his work as a carpenter and shipbuilder, a *faber navalis*. The lower inscription tells us that he is 'busy at work' and the accompanying relief shows him working to smooth a curved board for a ship that is still in drydock, its mast not yet in position. The monument is, in Clarke's words, 'an affront to elite taste', showcasing the details of manual labour which are conspicuously absent in memorials to members of the Roman upper classes. It shows us, by contrast, the lives of working-class Romans of differing status, in a place with strong Celtic roots, by no means entirely 'Roman' even at the end of the first century BCE. It shows their hard work, and the way that differing status was not necessarily a barrier to meaningful relationships of love and friendship.

From roughly the same period, or perhaps a few decades later, a similar artefact survives from the city of Rome, now in the collection of the Vatican Museums (see Figure 3a and 3b at the end of this chapter). It is an altar-ossuary, a memorial set up by a metalworker named Atimetus for himself and his colleague Epaphra, as well as their descendants. The marble altar functioned both as a memorial and as a place of repose for the bones of the deceased.

> Lucius Cornelius Atimetus [dedicates this altar] to himself and to Lucius Cornelius Epaphra, his meritorious freedman, and to the rest of his freedmen and freedwomen and to their descendants.

Atimetus and Epaphra were ironmongers who specialised in making knives. On either side of the altar are two reliefs of high quality, 'characteristic of many such monuments from the city of Rome', Clarke writes. The right side depicts a sales scene, in which a salesperson (presumably Atimetus) and a customer, both dressed in flowing togas, do business across a high-backed counter, with rows of knives hung up behind them. The left side is a scene from their workshop. Here you can see blades and tools hanging overheard, the anvil in the centre between the two men, and the outline of a bellows to the left. The man on the left sits side-on to the furnace, holding something in tongs so that it rests on an anvil; the man on the right is about to bring down a hammer, his muscular arm and the folds of his tunic shown in fine detail.

Each of these artefacts – the brooch, the tile, the memorials from Ravenna and Rome – show us the lives and work of ordinary people, and the pride those people took in their work. Their stories illuminate another side to life in ancient Italy, quite different from the lives of Rome's famous heroes, its poets and politicians, its wealthy elite. The story of Latin is, as we will explore further in Chapter 2, the story of artisans and craftspeople, people whose productive and creative labour produced objects of use and beauty, quite apart from wealth to be enjoyed by others. This is something that many of us are estranged from these days: the free use of labour to produce our own food, to produce and mend our own clothes, to repair and fix rather than throw out and buy again. Modern economic arrangements don't much value the work of artisans, and often export this kind of work to the poorest and most exploited parts of the world, where it can be done almost for free (made, that is, by paying the people who produce it next to nothing), and then sending it back to the wealthiest parts of the world where it is sold at great profit. Yet no matter where they live, humans have ways of connecting to seams of independent and creative labour, something professional artisans and tradespeople do every day. At the same time, it's important to remember that, then as now, the most backbreaking and dehumanising kinds of work are those most hidden away from polite society, and the historical record. For most Roman workers we have no evidence at all.

Before we leave the artisans, here is something that features no Latin whatsoever: a marble shop-sign from Ostia, dating from the second century CE, about one hundred years, perhaps, after the Ravenna and Roman memorials (see Figure 4 at the end of this chapter). Ostia was the port for the city of Rome, and in the second century was a bustling town of around 40,000 inhabitants. A woman stands behind her food-stall, handing a loaf of bread (or maybe a piece of fruit) to a customer. The stall is packed full of animals and produce: two pet monkeys, two caged hares. Some chickens – maybe

– poking their beaks through barred crates, pecking at the grain below. A wicker basket and, to its top left, a little snail, signifying its contents. Two dressed geese hanging upside down, ready for sale, and three customers, one of whom is, as mentioned, taking something from the shopkeeper's hand. There is no inscription to tell us the status of the woman: she could be a lowly employee, but, then again, she could be the proprietor. Her shop-sign gives an insight into something rarely seen in Latin literature: a street-scene from daily life, with all the hustle and bustle of a market morning. I've come across a similar moment in the classics only once – in Livy's *History of Rome* – when the Roman general Camillus enters the town of Tusculum and, expecting to find the place on a war-footing, is met instead with business as usual: women running errands, shopkeepers selling their wares, and schools 'full of the din of children learning'. The townspeople couldn't care less who this famous Roman general is, they're too busy getting on with their day. Just as if, I imagine, another proud Roman somebody approached this woman's shop in Ostia.

*

Imagine you are travelling from the south of Italy to Rome in ancient times. Unless you are someone important, you're likely travelling on foot, breaking the journey of many days into stages. The final part of the route takes you up the Appian Way, the main road into Rome from the south, and as you approach the city, stone tombs and memorials begin to line the road, as they did outside many Roman towns and cities. These memorials compete for your attention; they say things like 'Stop, traveller, and listen to my story', or 'Stay, read a while'. You might be glad of the rest. This is what a Roman graveyard looks like, and these inscriptions preserved on blocks of stone survive in great numbers from across the ancient Mediterranean. They speak to the influence of ancient Greece in Roman culture, where this kind of commemoration was first practiced, and, in their physicality, to a whole chain of production, including the person who commissioned the inscription, the person who arranged it on the stone, and finally the person who carved it. In 1885 a bilingual stone inscription was discovered in Sicily, advertising an ancient workshop where this kind of work was done: SIGNS HERE ARRANGED AND CARVED FOR HOLY BUILDINGS AND PUBLIC WORKS, just one example of what must have been a very common trade. The letter-forms found on these stones are famous and much replicated in modern visual culture, elegant capitals that are works of art in their own right.

As Ted Courtney explained, these inscriptions are interesting because, by their nature, they come from a much broader cross-section of society than the classic texts of Roman literature, 'from all social classes and every variety of occupation'. The stone that survives, if it survives, is the original artefact, whereas a famous Latin poem has been copied and corrected on manuscripts many times over: the original copy no longer exists. More importantly, these stones speak to the facts of life and death in moving ways; they are often written in verse and feature wordplay of different kinds, blurring the boundaries of what 'literature' is, and who it is for. Most of this evidence has been known about for centuries, it has been studied and preserved, and yet it has never enjoyed the same prestige or attention as the classics. Here is one found at Preturo near L'Aquila in central Italy, dating from the middle of the second century BCE. It commemorates the life of a man with a Greek name who, due to his trade, must have known Latin, perhaps employed by a wealthy Roman family.

> Protogenes, the genial mime-actor, slave of Cloelius, lies here; he gave the people great pleasure with his clowning.

And here is that of Marcus Caecilius:

This memorial was made for Marcus Caecilius.
Thank you, my dear guest, for stopping at my abode.
Good luck and good health to you. Sleep without a care.

This inscription appears to be from the same, second-century, period (although some have argued that it is later) and it features things that look strange to someone used only to later versions of the language. Marcus in the first line is MAARCO in Latin, with a double 'a' spelling taken from the Oscan language, while the last word is spelt with a q rather than the expected c (*qura*, not *cura*). The inscription is in verse, and, as Warmington notes in his translation, makes a play of imagining the monument as a house where you might stop in for chat. It is beautifully carved, with big clean capitals and dots to mark the spaces between the words.

We don't know who Marcus Caecilius was, what kind of status he enjoyed, or how he treated those around him. His inscription is found today in the complex of a much larger tomb, that of a Roman noblewoman called Caecilia Metella, on the Appian Way, a few miles south of Rome. Both Marcus and Caecilia share a Roman family name – that of the *gens Caecilia* – an old clan with several distinguished and powerful branches, so it's possible that Marcus was someone of importance, and that his inscription was originally part of a larger, grander, memorial. He's included in this story, however, because if he was, he – or whoever chose the words on his behalf – hasn't taken the trouble to tell us so. There is no mention, as there is in many other inscriptions, of rank, wealth, or career. Though privileged to have had a memorial made for him in the first place, and especially one that has survived, he is known to history only as Marcus Caecilius. The simplicity and warmth of his greeting shine through.

Evidence for the lives of Roman women is often scarce, so it is especially valuable. Here is a memorial to Claudia, again originally in verse, and again dating from the middle of the second century BCE:

> Stranger, my message is short. Stand by and read it through. Here is the unlovely tomb of a lovely woman. Her parents called her Claudia by name. She loved her husband with her whole heart. She bore two sons; of these she leaves one on earth; under the earth has she placed the other. She was charming in conversation, yet proper in bearing. She kept house, she made wool. That's my last word. Go your way.

There is the same direct address to the passer-by, sterner this time, and a triple wordplay in the Latin: between lovely (*pulchrum*), unlovely (*haud pulchra*) and the word for tomb (*sepulcrum*). Most of the inscription is written in the third person, only switching to the first person in the final two words (literally: 'I have spoken, go away'). Claudia is represented as a wife, mother, and homemaker, an ideal Roman woman in the eyes of male society. Elements of the text, as in all inscriptions, may have been set phrases picked from a selection, much like when choosing a memorial today. We don't know what kind of life Claudia lived, whether she was able to live it on her own terms. Her wool-working can be taken as an idealised and stereotypical detail: it is what women are always doing in ancient literature, their signature occupation. Yet it also makes her an artisan, someone who spun and weaved, a creative producer of useful and beautiful things. The inscription tells us something about her humanity, her relationships, and the tragedy which marked her life. About the ways in which women, around the world, still tend to do a huge amount of unpaid and undervalued work.

One final group of inscriptions are memorials to children, like these ones to Mus ('Mouse'), who died aged thirteen, and Optatus ('Hoped for'), who died aged two and a half. Mouse's epitaph was found in Rome, while Optatus' was found several hundred years ago in the tower of a cathedral in southern Italy, by a scholar who copied it down before the original was lost.

> Dear to my loved ones, I passed away a young girl. Here I lie, dead: I am ash, and that ash is earth. But if the earth is a goddess, then I am a goddess, I am not dead. I ask you, traveller, not to disturb my bones. Mouse lived for thirteen years.
>
> Here lies Optatus, an infant known to all for his affection; I pray that his ashes be violets and roses, and that the earth, which is now his mother, be light on him, for the boy's life was oppressive to none. Therefore his wretched parents have set up this epitaph to their son, all that they can do.

For me these inscriptions are just as valuable and important as the famous literature of ancient Rome, and there is poetry in them. It's there in the children's names and what they mean, in the idea of Mother Earth now taking them back into her care after leaving their own, heartbroken, parents behind. They recall the fragility of human life, particularly in pre-modern times, and the miracle of a child surviving into adulthood. Most affecting of all is the idea of reincarnation, or perhaps regeneration, when Optatus' parents pray that his ashes become violets and roses. Courtney points out that Hamlet will wish something similar for his sister Ophelia in Shakespeare's play, a useful reminder to keep our ideas of poetry, and of literature, broad.

> Lay her in the earth;
> And from her fair and unpolluted flesh
> May violets spring!

*

Move now to the year 79 CE, when the towns of Pompeii and Herculaneum were buried by an eruption of Mt. Vesuvius. Since their rediscovery they've become perhaps the most famous Roman archaeological sites in the world, a time-capsule record of life on the Bay of Naples towards the end of the first century CE. Part cemetery, part open-air museum, they've been the subject of many books, films, and series. What is less well known is that on the walls and streets, and in the homes, of these towns, a huge amount of Latin has been preserved, important for being what Adams called 'the earliest substantial body of genuinely popular Latin' to survive intact. For me what's important about Pompeii and Herculaneum is this record left to us by a particular group of humans as they vied for business, went up for election, paid for sex, bought and sold slaves, declared their love, or simply etched their thoughts on a nearby wall. It's a relatively democratic body of evidence, which, owing to the nature of its creation, did not discriminate as to whose Latin, or which events, it preserved in ash. It's a reminder, therefore, of Latin as a language of everyday life, recording all kinds of human experience and behaviour.

You can see the townspeople of Pompeii in the wall-paintings that survive. These include glimpses of the ordinary town-folk, like the men and women walking in procession in honour of the goddess Cybele, the Great Mother, or the couple who, alongside their employees, combed wool and made it into cloth, to be sold in their adjoining shop. They are watched over by Venus in her guise as patron-goddess of the town, *Venus Pompeiana*. There are records of gladiatorial fights chalked on the walls – who won, who lost, who was set free – and, surviving from one tavern, a series of four paintings with text, appearing to show an argument between customers over a game of dice. Sometimes there is evidence of the earlier history of the town, from back in the time of the Social War, when the Oscan language still thrived, and Pompeii was besieged by a Roman army. Beneath a couple of layers of plaster a painting of four fighters was found, two on horseback, two on foot, with one name, in Oscan, still visible: it looks like 'Spartacus', leader of the famous slave revolt. Sometimes we have portraits of middle-class Pompeians that were completed just before the eruption, like the double portrait of a couple from a bakery complex. The man is holding a scroll and the woman a stylus and some wax writing-tablets, proudly showing us that they can read and write. Clarke notes that an image of Cupid and Psyche painted just above their portraits could have been intended as a symbol of their love. The portraits are realistic, warts-and-all, not perfect and model-like: they are shown as they were. (See Figure 5 at the end of this chapter.)

The walls, doorways, and pavements of Pompeii and Herculaneum are full of Latin. Signs that say things like 'Hail, Profit' or 'Profit, Joy', mosaics that warn you to beware of the dog (*cave canem*), and makeshift calendars telling you what the market days are in nearby towns: on Sundays it's at Cumae – no, wait – someone has crossed that out, it's Atilla and Nola. A doodle of a labyrinth with the words 'Here lives the Minotaur' beside it, or little dedications, like this one found in a kitchen:

> Felix [made] a vow to the household gods.

There are tongue-in-cheek apologies for wetting the bed ('Sorry, host! If you ask why: there was no pot'), and the lament of some exhausted tourists ('We came here eagerly; much more eager are we to go away'), while advertisements for a local favourite ('First-rate mackerel sauce of Marcus Acceius Telemachus') survive alongside notes on brothel walls and contracts for the sale of human beings (from Herculaneum: 'that [this] girl, who is mentioned above, is healthy, not charged with any theft or injurious conduct, and is not a runaway truant, is being handed over, and twice the price is being given, in accordance with the terms of the edict of the curule aediles . . . Gaius Iulius Phoebus has pledged . . .'). There are ironic tags that have been found at several different locations:

> I'm amazed, wall, that you haven't fallen down, since you carry the rubbish of so many writers!

and lovesick notes which others have come along and edited:

> Lovers, like bees, lead a honeyed life.
> (in another hand) I wish!

Graffiti is a useful kind of evidence because of its diverse and streetwise nature, representing real and often overlooked concerns. 'Young people need a dream' and 'Health is not a privilege: no one is expendable', on the streets of modern Naples, alongside fascist and anti-fascist slogans. 'The world would be nothing without females' proclaims a Dublin park-bench; 'Fugees Welcome' on a nearby wall.

Sometimes a piece of graffiti gives us an insight not just into ordinary life in Pompeii, but into lives that often go unrecorded in history. Like the tile signed by Detfri and Amica, they can help us to see those who are often overlooked. In 1888, a love poem was discovered scratched onto the doorway of a Pompeii house. What it appears to be, and what many people take it to be, is a love poem written by a woman to another woman; we know this because two of the relevant words in the inscription have feminine endings. There are, as always, more questions than answers, and lots of different possibilities. That this is a woman talking to herself and not to another woman, that this is a man adopting a woman's persona, that whoever wrote these lines on the wall was cobbling together quotations rather than creating original verse, and so on. The text is not as legible, or as easily interpretable, as we would like. You need to strike a balance between weighing up all these difficulties and realising that it's quite possible the text is what it appears to be. Here is the poem, in Ted Courtney's prose translation, slightly edited:

> Would that I might hold my arms embraced around your neck and give kisses with my tender lips. Go now, darling, and entrust your joys to the winds. Believe me, men's nature is fickle. When in my desperation I was lying awake in the middle of the night, often,

> thinking over things with myself, [I said]: 'Many whom Fortune has raised aloft, these she subsequently oppresses, suddenly hurled down headlong. Similarly, after Venus has suddenly united the bodies of lovers, daylight separates them . . .'

One way in which history can help is by showing that the lives people lead, no matter how unorthodox they might seem, no matter how 'unnatural' some would have us believe them to be, have been lived by others before us. If you know where to look, there's plenty of evidence for different kinds of love, and different kinds of sexuality, in historical sources from different parts of the world. It's something the ancient Greek and Roman worlds have always done well, complicating narrow and oppressive orthodoxies by showing us alternative ways of being. That larger point is worth remembering, whatever the difficulties in being certain about a particular piece of evidence.

*

Ever since the days of the Roman republic, Latin had been spreading beyond the Italian peninsula in tandem with the spread of the Roman state: first to places like Sicily and Spain, and eventually to much of the Mediterranean world. This meant the disappearance of other languages, languages with their own unique ways of seeing the world, as well as the imposition of a political system that was often ruthless and exploitative in its treatment of non-Roman communities. To talk about Latin is to realise the truth behind the saying that history is written by the victors. At the same time, language exists in the day-to-day, amidst and within larger political structures; it is reinvented (reappropriated, even) every time someone opens their mouth, or starts a conversation. 'this is the oppressor's language // yet I need it to talk to you', as Adrienne Rich puts it in her poem 'The Burning of Paper Instead of Children'. This is one of the paradoxes of Latin.

One place where a wealth of evidence for the language survives is Britain, occupied by the Roman state between the middle of the first and fifth centuries BCE. Between Cumbria and Newcastle, in the north of England, a series of Roman letters have come to light in excavations at the Roman army camp of Vindolanda. They were written in ink on frail sheets of birchwood, 'between 1 and 3mm thick and about the size of a modern postcard', Bowman notes, and survived in the oxygen-less conditions of the soil. They date from the decades either side of 100 CE and give a snapshot of life in the camp: predominantly, but not exclusively, the life of the men who staffed it as soldiers and commanders. These letters were first found only in the 1970s, and new ones have been published as recently as 2019. There are complaints about the weather and about the indigenous people just beyond the fence (the *Brittunculi*), letters of recommendation, quotations from Virgil, as well as requests from an officer to his superior for more beer (*cervesa*) for his men. They give us evidence for the Latin of ordinary people at the level of word as well as subject matter. The word used for horse in all the letters discovered so far is *caballus*, the forerunner of the Romance word (Fr. *cheval* etc.), but not the word found in classical Latin, which is *equus*. When *caballus* is used in classical Latin, it tends to refer to horses of inferior quality, but that would not have been the case for the army horses used at Vindolanda. 'Here is evidence', Adams wrote, 'for the social diversity of the language in the early second century. The man in the street used *caballus*, whereas high literature used *equus*. The everyday term remained largely submerged, but writing tablets have brought it to the surface and shown that it was not merely derogatory.'

Colonial garrison forts have existed in different colonial situations throughout history and across the world; they continue to exist today. I don't want to apologise for, or defend, their violent and oppressive function. I include the Vindolanda evidence here for a story that's at a tangent to, if not quite removed from, the mainstream of the Roman occupation. One of the letters that has survived is an invitation to a birthday party, from a woman named Claudia Severa to her friend Lepidina Sulpicia, both wives of soldiers stationed at the camp. Claudia has gotten a scribe to write the body of the letter, but has written the final bit in her own hand, an ancient surviving example of a woman's handwriting in Latin. Here is the translation given in the *Roman Inscriptions of Britain* database, slightly edited for clarity:

> First hand:
>
> Claudia Severa to her Lepidina greetings. On 11 September, sister, for the day of the celebration of my birthday, I give you a warm invitation to make sure that you come to us, to make the day more enjoyable for me by your arrival, if you are present. Give my greetings to your Cerialis. My Aelius and my little son send him their greetings.
>
> Second hand:
>
> I shall expect you, sister. Farewell, sister, my dearest soul, as I hope to prosper, and hail.

The language here is warm and affectionate, with the diminutive *filiolus* for 'my little son' and the word 'sister' (*soror*) a term of endearment rather than a family connection. It is full of things a reader of classical Latin does not expect: the k for c in *karissima* ('dearest'), the word *ave* ('hail') with a h at the front (*have*) and coming at the end rather than the beginning; the puzzle of 'as I hope to prosper', an unusual phrase not found elsewhere.

Claudia's letter is, more simply, evidence that ancient Roman people celebrated their birthdays and had birthday parties. Think about how you might write the sign-off at the end, and you'll see what I mean:

> Can't wait to see you! Bye for now, love, and chat soon x.

Then as now, a birthday is still cause for a party. Claudia and Sulpicia were privileged in some ways, and not in others. We don't know how they lived their lives, or what they thought about their position as part of a Roman garrison force. We can appreciate their humanity while remaining critical of the political situation they existed within.

One of the most famous sites in Roman Britain is the town of Bath, with its ancient ruins and its healing waters. Here, too, there survives evidence for the Latin of ordinary people. This time, it's a vindictive and bitter kind of language, the kind you'll be familiar with if you've ever had something stolen from you. All through the ancient life of the temple of Sulis Minerva at Bath, people scratched the name of a suspected thief and the object stolen (or paid someone to do it for them) on a tablet of lead alloy, which was then tossed into the waters of the temple in offering to the goddess, in hope of restoration or retribution. Over 130 tablets have been found at Bath, and more have come to light in places like Leicester and London in recent years; there are over 1,500 known across Europe, some in Greek and some in Latin. These are curse tablets, and, like the epitaphs discussed above, by their nature they were commissioned by a broad cross-section of society. Unlike the epitaphs, their language does not aspire to literary form, but reflects to some extent how people spoke.

Roman Bath was a multicultural place, something we can tell from the different kinds of artefacts found there (an Irish brooch; a memorial for the wife of a man from Palmyra, with some text in the Palmyrene language), and names of the people recorded on the tablets. In the Bath tablets, people complain about the theft of things like ploughshares, travelling cloaks, and a pair of gloves. The first curse tablet to be discovered in the town, back in 1880, relates to the theft of 'Vilbia'. It has been suggested that Vilbia is a Celtic name, referring to a girl, and if this is correct it's a grim but useful reminder of the trafficking that goes on in everyday life, then and now. There is something brutal about this evidence and the reality behind it. The tablet prays that the thief 'become liquid as water' and then names a list of potential suspects (in the tablet about the cloak, the vengeance is even scarier: death, insomnia, and infertility, all in a single curse). What's interesting from a linguistic point of view about the Vilbia tablet is the phrase, 'that [the thief] become as liquid as water', *ut liquat como aqua*. The word for the second 'as' in classical Latin is *quomodo*, but here it's written COMC, in what scholars think is *como* with *do* implied, so *comodo*. The q is written as a c, and the whole word has been shortened. What we have here, in other words, is a clear ancestor of the word for like or as in the Romance languages – Fr. *comme*, It. *come*, Sp. *como* etc. – hundreds of years before those languages were called as such. The implication being, that the *quomodo* of classical Latin had already changed in ordinary Latin long before the Romance languages appeared on the scene. As with Claudia's letter, some fascinating linguistic evidence needs to be kept in historical perspective. Everyday language encompasses the full range of human behaviour.

*

In 1884 a scholar named Gian Francesco Gamurrini discovered a manuscript in a library in Arezzo, Italy, containing an account, in Latin, of a woman's travels in the Holy Land. The beginning and the end of the account were missing, so her name and the dates of her journey were unclear. But subsequent work has come up with an informed guess at her name (Egeria) and a definite idea of when she travelled (between Easter 381 and Easter 384 CE). Egeria seems to have started from somewhere in the region of northern Spain or southern France, and she reached Jerusalem via Constantinople, staying there for an extended period and making excursions to places like Mt Sinai (Jabal Musa) in the Egyptian desert and the ancient city of Edessa, modern Urfa, in Turkey. Egeria writes to her 'reverend ladies, my sisters' back home, telling them in excited tones about the places she's been and the people she's met. She is a pilgrim, intent on seeing the sites she has read about in the Bible and visiting important churches and shrines. But she is also what we could call a tourist, and recounts her travels in ways very similar to how you or I would do when on holiday.

On her journey back to Constantinople she detoured to visit Edessa; she wanted to visit a shrine there to Thomas, the doubting apostle. To get there she had to cross the river Euphrates and noted that it was much bigger than the Rhône (a clue to her homeplace); on meeting her, the Bishop of Edessa was impressed that her faith had brought her 'right from the other end of the earth'. He took her to a local palace where she saw pools full of fish, and her next meal: 'they were so big, so brightly coloured, and tasted so good'. Earlier in her trip Egeria had climbed Mt. Sinai in the Egyptian desert – the steeper, more direct ascent, she tells us, rather than the easier, more circuitous route. At the summit she spoke with the community of monks living there and they gave her little gifts of the fruit they had grown; she looked down and admired the views, making sure to send a report back home:

> I want you to be quite clear about these mountains, reverend ladies, my sisters, which surrounded us as we stood beside the church looking down from the summit of the mountain in the middle. They had been almost too much for us to climb, and I really do not think I have ever seen any that were higher ... even though they only looked like hillocks to us as we stood on the central mountain. From there we were able to see Egypt and Palestine, the Red Sea and the Parthenian [i.e. the Mediterranean] Sea ... as well as the vast lands of the Saracens – all unbelievably far below us.

Like any tourist and pilgrim, Egeria was excited to be in places she had read about and were meaningful for her, and to share those experiences with those close to her. She is delighted when, travelling back through

Turkey, she runs into an old friend named Marthana from earlier in her trip. 'I simply cannot tell you', she writes, 'how pleased we were to see each other again.'

Egeria's account is an important one in the history of Latin. She is an independent and literate woman, one whose intellect and imagination are animated by her faith. Unlike the handful of other female pilgrims to the Holy Land we know about in this period, Egeria does not appear to have been an aristocrat; her Latin shows no signs of the education and high-style mannerisms that mark so much of the writing that survives from the medieval period. She is not trying to show off, or to write like Cicero, or to win an argument. Rather, she is writing in her own voice and painting a picture for her own religious community. The faults of style that, from a classical-scholarly perspective, mar her work are no faults at all, but a warm and vivid style of her own, and no less 'intellectual' for being so. As with the Bath curse tablet, what's interesting is that Egeria's Latin is full of elements that will later appear in the Romance languages. *Sabbato sera* ('late [on] Saturday/The Sabbath') and *septimana* ('week') are almost identical in modern Italian, while her blurring of the meaning of the verbs 'go' and 'be' (*ire* and *esse*) and her use of the verb *plicare* (in the sense 'to arrive') anticipate modern Spanish (*ser* and *irse*, *llegar*). In her account of the liturgical year in Jerusalem, meanwhile, she uses a pattern for the days of the week (*prima feria*, *secunda feria* etc.) that now belongs in modern Portuguese. As Adams noted, it's hard to take these details and build a definite picture about what Latin was spoken when and where, but the details in themselves are enough to showcase a down-to-earth and living language which, in all its variety, still exists today.

The Bible had been gradually translated into Latin in the two centuries prior to Egeria's trip, and while the circumstances of this process are not entirely clear to us, it seems to have begun in Roman North Africa. These were translations from Greek, which was the language of early Christian scripture: the Old Testament, originally in Hebrew, in its Greek translation known as the Septuagint, and the New Testament, originally written in Greek. In the same years that Egeria was travelling in the Holy Land, a scholar known to history as St Jerome revised the Latin translation of the Gospels according to both the existing Latin versions and the Greek text, at the request of Pope Damasus I: there is a copper engraving by Albrecht Dürer (1471–1528) in which you can see the saint busy at work, hunched over his desk with good light streaming in through the window. In later years, Jerome would go on to produce a new translation of much of the Old Testament too, bypassing the Greek version and going back to the Hebrew text, and together his translations would constitute the standard Latin version of the Bible for centuries to come. In its early life, however, the Latin Bible was more about pragmatism than prestige, and the older, pre-Jerome translations existed side-by-side with his version for many centuries. As with Egeria, my interest here is not with the dogma and power structures of religious elites, but with literature as a facet of everyday life and popular culture.

Latin has been at different times in its Christian life a language of religious orthodoxy and terror, both in Europe and in the European empires abroad. *Extra ecclesiam nulla salus*, or 'outside the Church there is no salvation', as the saying goes. The Latin Bible has an imposing and sometimes dismaying history, better known from the perspective of the Reformation, when the demand was for Bibles in languages which people actually spoke and could understand; when the Latin tide was going out. But if you go back to its beginnings in the first centuries of Christianity, the Latin Bible was itself a translation from more prestigious languages, meant to give Latin speakers of all stripes access to its stories. People who could then decide for themselves which of those stories were useful and meaningful to them, and which weren't. The Latin of the Bible is in one sense a bespoke language, full of the influence of Greek and Hebrew and special religious terminology. In another sense, though, the simplicity of its storytelling reinvented what literature meant in Latin, because by any previous definition of that word it fell far short. Jerome was careful to preserve this simplicity when revising the New Testament, and to maintain it when translating the Old. He could easily have adopted a more 'classical' style, akin to the authors of ancient Rome, but he chose not to so that the work would be understood as widely as possible.

The Latin Bible throughout its life has spoken to popular concerns. The Book of Ruth, for instance, is the story of two women – one of them an outsider – in a difficult situation. At times, the language used is very simple, as when Ruth tells Naomi: *populus tuus populus meus, et deus tuus deus meus.*

> Your people will be my people and your God my God.

I first came across Ruth's story in a poem by the Irish poet Eiléan Ní Chuilleanáin, entitled 'To Niall Woods and Xenya Ostrovskaia, Married in Dublin on 9 September 2009'. As the title suggests, it's a wedding poem, and it features a cat who speaks Irish and Russian. This cat knows many tales, but there is one he doesn't – the book of Ruth – so the poet lends him a hand. Or take the story of the Nativity in the Gospel of Luke, when the shepherds arrive and tell the new parents about seeing the choir of angels on their journey to greet the baby Jesus. The story gives Mary a moment to herself, in a way I hadn't noticed until one of my students pointed it out. One of the most spoken-for women in history is given her own inner life, to which the reader has no access, as she takes it all in.

> But Mary treasured up all these things and pondered them in her heart.

Finally, consider the moment in the Gospel of Matthew when a storm comes in over the Sea of Galilee, and Jesus appears to the terrified disciples to reassure them:

> Take courage! It is I. Don't be afraid.

A few years ago, in Bulgaria for a friend's wedding, my friends and I visited the forested hills above Sofia. There is a church there known as the Boyana Church, a UNESCO World Heritage Site with its origins in the tenth century CE, where the medieval frescoes reminded me of this moment. One of them dramatises St Nicholas calming some sailors much as Jesus does here, the sea done in big swirls of blue and the saint standing calmly in the bow, a halo on his head.

The Latin in the Gospel for 'don't be afraid' is *nolite timere*. In a story that is now quite well-known, these words featured in a text message the Irish poet Seamus Heaney (1939–2013) sent to his wife, Marie, just before he died. Heaney had learnt Latin at school, and knew to use the singular version of the phrase rather than the plural: *noli timere*. Those words were then made into a giant mural by the artist Maser in December 2013, still there in Dublin's Portobello, and in English rather than in Latin: DON'T BE AFRAID. I was cheered to see how many translations the text had been through (Greek, Latin, English; the Bible, a text message, a Dublin wall), how it was there to give beleaguered commuters a lift during a rainy Dublin winter at the height of a deep recession. You might get the reference, or you might simply appreciate the words by themselves, a moment of encouragement. Recently I saw *noli timere* on a poster of Seamus Heaney above a Galway shop, this time kept in its original Latin, doing the same job. If Latin is a language of stories, those stories are only as positive or as negative, as useful or as dangerous, as the people who tell them and listen to them. There are many radical branches to the Christian story, people who took issue with the injustices of the organised church and were proudly heretical, sometimes at the expense of their lives. The Bible, too, has a radical side to it, and has always been part of the imaginative lives of ordinary people. A couple of summers ago, when standing outside the Cathedral in Milan, I overheard a mother passing with her young son; she was holding him by the hand and telling him fondly how 'Noah put *all* the animals into the ark . . .'. That is the kind of thing I mean.

If you think about Latin in terms of human history, the twenty-first century is not so distant from the people who appear in this chapter. The human species is about 300,000 years old; agriculture about 10,000, while the famous cave-paintings of Lascaux in France and Altamira in Spain date from around 15,000 and 12,000 years ago respectively. The anthropologist David Graeber (1961–2020) once wrote about 'blowing up walls', criticising 'the arrogant, unreflecting assumption which tells us we have nothing in common with 98% of people who ever lived, so we don't really have to think about them.' Graeber was criticising the idea that 'modernity' is something which happened at some point between the seventeenth and nineteenth centuries, in Western Europe and its settler colonies, which makes those who lived before that time fundamentally different to those of us who live now. As he makes clear, his critique is not some naïve argument for making everyone and everything the same: every individual, never mind every historical situation, is unique. But he recognises with others that history, if it is to be useful, is about making connections. If you're lucky enough to have been able to visit the sites of Pompeii and Herculaneum, you'll know the strange jolt you get when seeing the plaster casts of the humans and animals who died in the eruption, frozen at the moments of their deaths. Their world was more fragile and more endangered than they knew. In the different ways they lived, and the different ways they spoke, I can't help but think of them as familiar.

Figure 1 *The Palestrina brooch © The Center for Epigraphical and Palaeographical Studies, The Ohio State University.*

Figure 2 *The memorial to Longidienus and his family © By permission of the Italian Ministry of Culture – Regional Directorate of the Museums of Emilia-Romagna.*

Figure 3a *The altar-ossuary of Atimetus and Epaphra, right side (sales scene)*

Figure 3b *The altar-ossuary of Atimetus and Epaphra, left side (workshop scene)*

Figure 4 *A shop-sign from ancient Ostia © Digital image courtesy of the American Academy in Rome, Photographic Archive.*

Figure 5 *A portrait from Pompeii © By permission of the Italian Ministry of Culture – National Archaeological Museum, Naples – photo by Giorgio Albano.*

2

Pop Classics

Latin is famous for its classics, the poetry and prose that survives from a small window in the history of the language between about 200 BCE and 200 CE. No ancient copies of these works survive, so we owe our ability to read them at all to another aspect of Latin's human chain: the monks, scribes, and scholars – most of them anonymous – who copied texts they valued from manuscript to manuscript, editing and correcting as best they could. We're lucky to have the work of Catullus, for instance, the poet from Verona whose poems survived into the medieval period in a single manuscript, which surfaced in his hometown in the thirteenth century. It then disappeared again, but not before it had been copied at least twice. One of these copies, now in the Bodleian Library in Oxford, is the single thread along which his poetry made it to the modern world. Catullus can be famously romantic and famously obscene; like his predecessor and inspiration Sappho he writes well about love and loss. In one of his long poems, he retells the story of the marriage of Peleus and Thetis, the parents of Achilles, and sets within it the story of Theseus and Ariadne. Like many ancient Roman poems, this one is full of Greek mythology in ways that can make it seem intimidating. But that would be to underestimate the brilliance of what Catullus can do, weaving together a story full of colour and romance in ways that remind me of the stained-glass windows of Harry Clarke (1889–1931). For one of his own masterpieces, Clarke, like Catullus, chose a very literary subject matter, in his case a John Keats poem called 'The Eve of St. Agnes'. If you go to the Hugh Lane Gallery on Dublin's Parnell Square and see the window up close, you'll see the magical craftsmanship, all deep blues and pinks, with which Clarke treats his subject, doing in glass what Catullus does in words.

Sometimes a work survives only in fragments, like the bits of an ancient Roman novel attributed to a courtier of the emperor Nero. This is the *Satyricon*, one long fragment of which describes a lavish and boozy Roman dinner party hosted by wealthy ex-slave, or freedman, called Trimalchio. It's interesting to scholars of the Latin language because its author, at different points in the story, has made a deliberate effort to reproduce the everyday language in which people spoke. From a reader's point of view, however, the interest is all in what happens at this strange evening. The guests are treated to the idiosyncratic behaviour of their host and to a whole range of exotic dishes: starters done in the twelve signs of the zodiac, and a pig wearing a freedman's cap, roasted and stuffed with live thrushes. As the evening goes on and the wine keeps flowing, there is gossip and storytelling, pranks and amateur dramatics, as appearance and reality begin to blur together. It's only when the fire-brigade arrive thinking that the house is on fire that the narrator and his friend decide to hit the road. Just before this, Trimalchio had been discussing his will, and his plans for his tomb, much to the distress of his guests:

> Put a sundial in the middle, so that whoever wants to know the time will read my name, whether he wants to or not. Oh yes, and give some thought to whether this inscription strikes you as suitable enough:

> *Here rests Gaius Pompeius Trimalchio of the household of Maecenas. He was formally declared Priest of Augustus in his absence. Though he could have claimed membership of every Roman guild, he refused. He was god-fearing, brave, and faithful. He grew from small beginnings and left thirty million, and he never heard a philosopher lecture. Farewell, Trimalchio; and fare well, you who read this.*
>
> As he uttered these words, Trimalchio began to weep copiously. Fortunata too wept, and so did Habinnas. In fact the whole household filled the dining room with cries of grief, as though summoned to a funeral. By now even I had begun to blub, when Trimalchio said: 'So since we know that our death is in the offing, why don't we enjoy life?'

Like many Latin works, Petronius' novel has had a big influence on later writers and artists, particularly in the twentieth century. You'll find it used at the front of T. S. Eliot's *The Waste Land* (1922), for instance, and on screen in a version by Federico Fellini (1969). But where the work really shines is as a major influence on F. Scott Fitzgerald's *The Great Gatsby* (1925), which, right up until the last minute, was due to be called *Trimalchio in West Egg*. There are lots of similarities between the two works, which can help to illuminate them both: a naïve but observant narrator, a mysteriously wealthy host, a raucous social set, a sense of after-hours nihilism, and appearances that deceive. Both works hold a mirror up to high society, leaving you to draw conclusions about the character and morals of that society, but only if you want to.

Sometimes not only does a work survive by the skin of its teeth, or in fragments, but with question marks as to its authenticity. This is the case with the poetry of Sulpicia, the only woman in the canon of classical Latin poetry, whose place is not universally accepted. That's because Sulpicia's poems survive jumbled up in the manuscript tradition of another poet, and were only identified as being hers by a scholar in the nineteenth century. Definitive proof is not forthcoming, but there are scholars who point out that the poems could very well be what they appear to be – the work of a young Roman noblewoman, writing in the 20s BCE – and that believing them to be so requires only the same considered act of faith accorded to every other ancient author.

At last: here's love. Not to be kept quiet, either,
but shouted from the rooftops without shame.
Venus and the Muses have answered my prayers
and put him in my lap. Yes, Venus has kept her word:
here's joy for you, all you without your own!
Not for me those sealed tablets to keep our notes
from prying eyes: it's a thrill to fall, a pain to play the lady.
Well-matched, my man and me, is what they'll say.

Sulpicia's poems put me in mind of the great jazz singers of the twentieth century, in their breezy assertion of romantic independence: Nina Simone singing Bessie Smith's *I Want a Little Sugar in My Bowl*, or Etta James' *At Last*.

A full list of the Latin classics would include many more authors than I discuss here; a great many works haven't survived at all. A pessimistic reading of their history would recognise that they have often been for some people and not for others: taught in expensive schools and universities and found on the reading lists of imperialists and fascists right up to the present day. Taken as a collection of works, Latin literature is limited in its interests and concerns because of the narrow social context in which it was first produced and read: the high society of ancient Rome. Yet this isn't the whole story. There is another side to Latin literature that is popular and plural, messy and creative, functioning through the ages as a kind of grab-bag for readers and artists and writers of many different stripes. Ancient Roman culture has always been public property, whenever someone uses a phrase like 'crossing the Rubicon' or 'all roads lead to Rome'; whenever someone picks up a paperback Catullus or a book on Roman history; whenever someone flicks on to a documentary about Pompeii and keeps watching, or wonders why the Romans never came to Ireland. The history of Latin literature is in part a history of ordinary readers, most of them unknown, and its works can still speak to everyday concerns. In this chapter I'd like to try and show you how.

*

Let's begin quite early, around the year 200 BCE, with the first Latin author whose work has survived in a complete form. This is Plautus, a writer of comedies that were put on in Rome but set in Greece, who translated and adapted Greek originals for his Roman audience, borrowing much, but adding lots of his own stuff too. Plautus is definitely one of the classics – held up by one ancient critic as one of the best writers of all – but he's also a bit of an outlier, not just in terms of when he wrote but in terms of his style. These days most students of Latin tend to stick to authors from a later period, either side of the year 0 CE, when the writing is often quite formal. So it can be a something of a challenge if and when they encounter the text of one of Plautus' plays, which, though stylised in their own way, are full of dialogue and people talking to each other. Not in the rhetorical and highly dramatic way they do in Virgil or Seneca, but in the back-and-forth nattering of everyday conversation. If you want the Latin for 'how's it going', 'please', and 'go away', you go to Plautus, and it was a small shock to me to find in his plays a real sense of what the language must have sounded like in the streets and markets of ancient Italy. Think of a cross between Shakespeare, Stephen Sondheim, and a

Christmas pantomime and you'll have some idea of his style. His language is glittering and over-the-top, full of puns and jokes and wordplay, conversational and elevated at the same time. He introduced lots of music to the plays which does not survive. And his characters are a gang of pompous generals, bumbling fathers, promising young men and at-risk young women, larger-than-life caricatures meant to amuse the crowd and take a few of them down a peg.

I've been referring to Plautus as the single author of his plays, but this is one of the many things which remain uncertain, and not just because a play is much more than a script, and scripts are all we have. Where were they performed? Who by, and for whom? And how did they go down with the audience? The traditional view has been that Plautus was a writer and actor from Umbria, that the plays were put on at festivals in make-shift outdoor theatres beneath the steps of a temple (or temples) in the city of Rome. That in the audience were, by and large, the Roman upper classes enjoying a night off, and that the content was supposed to send them up gently while reassuring them that the status quo was here to stay. Where things get interesting is in relation to the central role in most of the plays, the character to whom Plautus gives the best plots and best lines. This character is a male slave, who runs rings around his master and most of the rest of the cast, is full of bravado and intelligence and almost always manages to escape the punishment that's due. The question is how could, from an elite point of view, such a dangerous character – an independent slave in a slave-owning society – be given such a voice, and the answer is usually that in the festival atmosphere in which the plays were performed, there was a kind of one-night-only relaxation of normal expectations, with everything to be back in its oppressive place the next morning. Further questions include whether or not there were real-life slaves in the casts and in the audiences, and whether Plautus himself was in fact a single author, or just a name behind the genre, as it were.

You might characterise the standard interpretation, then, as culture from above: the plays were put on by and for Rome's upper class, and, while they might have sometimes seemed dangerously satirical, they ultimately kept everyone else in their place. The unfree characters had their bit of freedom on stage, but their real-life counterparts did not. Recently, however, a scholar named Amy Richlin has turned this view on its head, in an extended argument which I'd like to share with you here. Richlin argues that Plautine theatre can be understood as slave theatre, a collaborative practice by actors who, many of them slaves themselves, were 'highly skilled but socially marginal'. In a war-torn society full of hunger, deprivation, and human trafficking, as the Italy of the time was, troupes of actors used their art to vent their frustrations and keep themselves going, expressing anger at the conditions of their lives as well their inherent dignity, all the while keeping the memory and possibility of freedom, in its various forms, alive. They performed not only in the city of Rome but toured the surrounding towns, to audiences that were considerably more mixed than the traditional account holds. If the casts were all male, as it is assumed, then the female roles meant a kind of drag, with all the possibility for what Irish drag queen Panti Bliss calls 'gender discombobulation' that goes with it. That the plays were set in Greece, and not Rome, gave the cast some leeway: they could send up and critique their bumbling masters and their idiot sons, they could give full voice to their humanity in spite of their social status, and then use the Greek setting as a kind of insurance: well, you needn't really worry because we're not talking about here, are we? Certain elements of Richlin's argument are uncontroversial – about the status of actors in Rome, or the cross-dressing male cast – but overall, it amounts to a significant departure.

Richlin's argument is important because it helps us to see that there is nothing inevitably right about the view, built up over many centuries, that these plays are meant to make us relate to the masters and the slave-owners more than to the slaves; by contrast it highlights the bias of scholarship. One of the blind-spots of European intellectual history, writes Cornel West, has been its 'inability to believe in the capacities of oppressed people to create cultural products of value and oppositional groups of value', and so to make the connection between artistic practice and political consciousness. Richlin compares Plautus' plays to America in the time of slavery. Here too art was a means by which an oppressed people, in terrible circumstances, expressed their anger as well as their hope, and kept the idea of freedom alive. Here too, as with the Greek setting for Plautus' plays, a kind of double-speak gave people an opportunity to disguise the true meaning of their art. Songs that spoke of the River Jordan and Canaan were used as code for rivers and promised lands much closer to home. Here is Frederick Douglass, reflecting on a period before a failed escape attempt, in lines quoted by Richlin:

> We were, at times, remarkably buoyant, singing hymns and making joyous exclamations, almost as triumphant in their tone as if we had reached a land of freedom and safety. A keen observer might have detected in our repeated singing of
>
> 'O Canaan, sweet Canaan,
> I am bound for the land of Canaan'
>
> something more than a hope of reaching heaven. We meant to reach the *north* – and the north was our Canaan.

We can't travel back in time to observe the plays first-hand, and all arguments about them necessarily lack the final proof: we only have the scripts, which themselves were first collected in the form we have them decades after Plautus' death. It's telling that the American context has also been used to argue in the other direction: that Plautus' plays were the equivalent of the minstrel shows which made slave-characters famous, while the misery of real-life slaves continued unrelentingly.

The final verdict comes down to each reader. The plays are not perfect, and their practitioners were not saints. There are misogynistic jokes, and the plot of one of the most well-known plays, *The Pot of Gold*, involves the rape of a citizen girl (unlike the plays of Terence, which I discuss below, this play is not interested in exploring the consequences of sexual violence in meaningful ways). Though often bawdy and sometimes distasteful, the plays are not pornographic; they put on stage life as it is, not as we might like it to be. At the same time, they speak truth to many different kinds of power: abusive fathers and presumptuous adolescent boys, greedy pimps and deluded soldiers, the misery of gender stereotypes and the evil of slavery. In *The Ghost*, a slave named Tranio tricks his businessman master into buying a house from his neighbour, ostensibly to give his son a hand-up onto the property ladder, but really to pay for the freedom of a woman the son is seeing; Tranio avoids any punishment by hopping up onto an altar at the end, where he is, by law, immune. In *Captives*, a slave-owner is struck by the friendship between a master and his slave, both prisoners of war, and by how warmly the slave praises his master. He's a figure of ridicule here, as the audience knows that master and slave have swapped identities in order to escape, as the whole idea of 'natural' slavery is sent up. At times female characters are given just enough time on stage to speak their own truth to power, like the unnamed girl character in *Persa* who asks her father why he is selling her, or a slave named Syra in *The Merchant*, who complains about the hypocrisy of men, able to sleep around unpunished while women who do the same are divorced in a heartbeat. If the roles were reversed, she tells the audience in a brief soliloquy, 'I'd bet there would now be more divorced men than women.'

For some this kind of content isn't enough to rescue the material from an oppressively elite and patriarchal place; I would counter that good drama can do a lot of things at once, and if you allow space for both realism (this isn't a utopia) and performance (on which so much of a play's meaning depends), the plays' radical potential becomes clearer. There must have been so much street-performance in ancient Rome, most of which we can only outline in the faintest terms. Plautus brings to life the speech and streets of that city, and thereby connects us to a human past.

Another of the plays is called *The Rope*, about a young woman who is abducted from Athens by someone who wants to traffic and exploit her. But the ship in which the abductor is taking his captives to Sicily sinks in a great storm off the coast of Libya, where the woman, Palaestra, and her friend, Ampelisca, wash up safely on shore. They call to each other in the conversational Latin often found in Plautus:

> **Palaestra** Why don't I call her by her name so that she can hear me? (*Loudly.*) Ampelisca!
>
> **Ampelisca** Ha! Who is it?
>
> **Palaestra** It's me, Palaestra.
>
> **Ampelisca** Tell me, where are you?
>
> **Palaestra** Goodness, right now I'm in very many troubles.
>
> **Ampelisca** I'm your partner: my share isn't smaller than yours. But I'm keen to see you!

The storm had been raised by the star Arcturus, who opens the play – imagine a man with a star on his head coming out on stage – and tells us that he sees all human action, rewarding the good and punishing the bad: the world of this play is a moral one, however imperfect. Palaestra's former boyfriend has arrived to search, and there is an old man, himself an exile from Athens, who sees the storm from dry land and makes to help the women. Despite the attentions of both, the women are clearly the agents of their own rescue, and find shelter with a local priestess.

A slave named Gripus, meanwhile, has found a trunk in the sea when out fishing, which will turn out to contain Palaestra's belongings; it has him dreaming of the money he will get for it, and the possibility of his freedom. It will transpire that this trunk contains tokens by which Palaestra will realise that the old man from Athens, Daemones, is her long-lost father. Palaestra's line, in particular, has a music to it that's hard to reproduce in English: *salve,* she says, *mi pater insperate.*

Palaestra Greetings to you, my unhoped for father.

Daemones Greetings. How happy I am to embrace you!

Gripus, though not without a significant amount of hard bargaining, ends the play with his freedom. You can read *The Rope* in different ways, but for me it's a kind of redemption song, full of humane imagination and political possibility. Shakespeare was heavily influenced by Plautus, and took something of *The Rope* for *The Tempest*, another play which opens with a storm at sea.

*

There is one other writer of comedies from ancient Rome whose work survives in a complete form. This is Terence, who wrote and staged six plays in the 160s BCE. As scholars often note, the world of Terence's plays is quite different to that of Plautus. There is less slapstick physical comedy, less Roman detail intruding into the Greek setting, and less interest in making the character of the slave the hero. If Plautus is Shakespeare then Terence is Oscar Wilde. Everyday conversation is elevated to the point where it is a work of art in its own right, but never quite losing its connection to how people speak:

> I hope, Cecily, I shall not offend you if I state quite frankly and openly that you seem to me to be in every way the visible personification of absolute perfection.

Like Wilde, Terence was, according to tradition, a newcomer in a society he made fun of on stage: the line between comedy and satire is always a fine one. Terence's plays, like those of Plautus, are based on Greek originals and feature sexual violence in their plots, though this is never portrayed directly onstage. This can make them seem distant and strange to some readers, but for me they always seem modern. They remind me of famous middle-class family dramas from the last two centuries, like Ibsen's *Hedda Gabler* or Tennessee Williams' *Cat on a Hot Tin Roof*. In these plays a crisis unfolds which threatens to ruin an entire family and – even worse – its reputation in polite society. The playwright is interested in what really happens, not the images of themselves people like to present. As when the stunned judge at the end of *Hedda Gabler* mutters how 'people just don't do such things', or when Brick's mother asks Elizabeth Taylor – in the 1958 film version of *Cat on a Hot Tin Roof* – whether she 'makes Brick happy', the real question being: why do I have no grandchildren yet? If the plays are shocking, it's in service of the truth.

This is something done brilliantly in Terence's *The Mother-in-Law*, which in its use of suspense and who-knows-what-when feels more like a thriller than a comedy. A young man is in crisis because he has discovered that his new wife is pregnant and he isn't the father: he knows this because they haven't slept together. Before his marriage, we also learn, he had broken up with a woman, a sex worker, he was happy with, in order to comply with his father's wishes that he settle down with a suitable match. The first half of the play is all about setting up Pamphilus as a promising and noble young man, doing his best and hit with misfortunes he couldn't have predicted. His new wife has gone back to live with her parents, and everyone wastes little time in blaming the mothers-in-law. Terence writes characters with more depth than Plautus; he is interested in what people go through and how they treat each other, as in these lines where a slave and a sex worker are catching up:

> **Parmeno** Tell me, Philotis, where have you been enjoying yourself all this time?
>
> **Philotis** I've scarcely been enjoying myself, I tell you, having left here for Corinth with that brute of a soldier and endured two whole years of misery with him.

The Latin is more expressive than the English here: this solider was *inhumanissimus* in his treatment of Philotis. In one word Terence gets across the history of an abusive relationship, and makes us see it from the woman's point of view.

As the action continues, Terence skilfully dismantles the audience's expectations, and our positive opinion of Pamphilus. The mothers-in-law are blameless, and Philumena is pregnant due to rape, perpetrated by an unknown attacker nine months before (the baby has just been born). It will turn out that Pamphilus is the rapist. He had stolen Philumena's ring and given it as a present to Bacchis, his ex, on whose finger it has now been spotted by Philumena's mother. Bacchis pieces everything together and tells Pamphilus. This is shocking on many levels: the violence of the rape itself, that Philumena has borne her rapist's child and is now married to him, that Pamphilus and Bacchis decide to keep the truth to themselves at the end of the play. But while it may be shocking it portrays nothing that doesn't happen in real life. In the 2021 Pedro Almodóvar film *Parallel Mothers*, there is, as in Terence's play, a slightly contrived premise, in this case that two babies have been swapped at birth in a modern Spanish maternity hospital. But this set-up works because, once you enter into it, it allows the filmmaker to tell a story about injustice in a powerful way, including the injustices perpetrated against women in patriarchal society. As in *The Mother-in-Law*, sexual violence is central to the plot: we learn halfway through the film that one of the central characters was gang-raped and gave birth to a child as a result. Terence and Almodóvar both set out to shock the audience with the mundane brutality of sexual violence; this is neither voyeuristic nor gratuitous, but to make the audience reflect. Violence against women remains endemic around the world, with high-profile rape trials making headlines in both Spain and Ireland in recent years. *The Mother-in-Law* is a nightmare dressed up as a comedy, and all the more powerful for being so.

What do we know about Terence? There is an ancient biography which tells us that he was from north Africa, what is now Tunisia, and that he was a slave in the household of a Roman nobleman. This nobleman freed Terence because of his talent and his good looks; he wrote plays and died young, perhaps before the age of thirty. This ancient biography dates from many years after Terence lived, and his life-story, including the detail that he was from north Africa, is treated very sceptically by most scholars. Even the fact that Terence's name seems to recall his birthplace – Publius Terentius *Afer* – could be simply a coincidence. Yet the possibility that Terence, one of the most famed Latin authors, was an ex-slave from north Africa, has been of more than academic interest to many of his readers. The poet Phillis Wheatley (1753–84) was trafficked from West Africa as a child and shipped across the Atlantic to Boston, where she was bought to serve as a slave in the household of a Boston merchant named John Wheatley. She learnt Latin, translated Ovid, and was the first African American to publish a book in the colonies, a book of poems for which she was granted her freedom. I don't want to celebrate the culture of the slave-owning world into which she was brought against her will. This is Latin as the master's language. And yet that's not the whole truth either, because Phillis used her gifts for language to shape her own destiny.

The colonial American state was built on an imagined inheritance from Greece and Rome – think of how aggressively the architecture of the US Capitol in Washington DC imitates ancient temples – and this was used to justify its colonial expansion and its slave economy. But Wheatley, as John Levi Barnard has argued, is one of many African-American writers and artists who refused to leave Greece and Rome to the powerful and unscrupulous ruling classes. In her first published poem, she addresses the famous patron of Rome's most famous poets, Maecenas, and proudly takes her place among them. She name-checks Terence specifically, a footnote in the first edition leaving readers in no doubt about the connection: 'He was African by birth'. In a racist society Wheatley made the classics her own, raised her voice, and so inaugurated a long and radical tradition. Two centuries later Langston Hughes (1902–67), poet of the Harlem Renaissance, traced African-American history back to earliest human times, in a poem titled 'Prelude to Our Age: A Negro History Poem'. Terence is there, so is Phillis Wheatley, alongside Aesop and Sheba and the Egyptian Pharaohs, the music of southern Spain and the prayers of Western Africa; so too is Juan Latino of Granada, the famous sixteenth-century Latin scholar.

In our own times, the writer and poet Maya Angelou (1928–2014) also took inspiration from Terence, in particular a famous line from one of his plays, which goes

homo sum: nihil humani a me alienum puto

or, in English, 'I am a human being: I consider nothing human alien to me.'

The line in the original play is spoken by a busybody neighbour defending his snooping. There's something lovely in the way it has been taken out of context ever since as a motto for humane understanding, one more case of reimagination. You can watch a video of Angelou online, explaining what the verse means to her. For someone who has always struggled with how Latin should sound (more on this in Chapter 3) it was a thrill to hear her chant the line aloud with the voice and cadence for which she was famous. This is poetry, I thought. Here is a little bit of what she says.

> I'd like everybody to think of a statement by Terence. The statement is: 'I am a human being: nothing human is alien to me'. If you can internalise at least a portion of that, you will never be able to say, of an act, a criminal act, 'oh I couldn't do that'. No matter how heinous the crime, if a human being did it, you have to say I have in me all the components that are in her, or in him; I intend to use my energies constructively, as opposed to destructively. If you can do that about the negative, just think what you can do about the positive.

Think back to the soldier in *The Mother-in-Law* who was *inhumanissimus*, a brute. Angelou, like Terence, is interested in the full spectrum of human behaviour, our ability to be horrible to each other, as well as our potential for heroism and love. She is part of the same tradition as Wheatley, Hughes, and what Cornel West calls the 'Afro-American spiritual-blues impulse' we looked at in relation to Plautus. There is nothing naively optimistic here: any hope is hard won, and has taken full look at the worst. This is the freedom that James Baldwin writes about when talking about gospel and jazz, the freedom of those who have 'been down the line'. I think I find it in the works of Plautus and Terence.

*

Virgil's *Aeneid* was left almost complete on the poet's death in 19 BCE. It tells the story of Aeneas, a refugee fleeing the city of Troy on the north-western coast of Turkey, and his journey across the Mediterranean with a band of survivors from the Trojan War. Meeting disaster after disaster, they make their way westward, eventually arriving on the coast of Italy near the city of Rome. The poem is famous for the adventures of its first half: the fall of Troy and the Greeks in the wooden horse, the love of Queen Dido and Aeneas, and the hero's journey underground to visit the shade of his dead father. It is full of moments that have been loved by generations of readers, like when Dido realises that she is falling in love again after promising herself she never would. 'I feel again a spark of that former flame', she confesses to her sister, Anna. It is also full of moments which predict the future glory and greatness of Aeneas' descendants, the Roman empire, and the family line which the emperor Augustus, in Virgil's own time, will claim as his own. For Seamus Heaney, who translated the sixth book of the poem, it was 'the best and worst of books':

> Best because of its mythopoeic visions, the twilit fetch of its language, the pathos of the many encounters it allows the living Aeneas with his familiar dead. Worst because of its imperial certitude, its celebration of Rome's manifest destiny and the catalogue of Roman heroes.

That imperial certitude is something some readers love, others find difficult, even repulsive. There have always been readers who have identified more closely with those who are left behind by, defeated by, or opt out of, Aeneas' mission.

It's important, if you do read the *Aeneid*, to read the second half. That's because it's there that the dream of future glory is complicated by what happens. Aeneas has been promised a permanent home in Italy and a glorious future for his people. Not only is it unclear how much of this divine messaging he understands, but everything begins to fall to pieces. There are indigenous Italian peoples who are unwilling to be walked over by the new arrivals, while the hero becomes more and more brutalised by the effects of war. During the fall of Troy Aeneas was compared to an unwitting shepherd, shocked by the speed and vehemence of an approaching bushfire; by the poem's final book he is again a shepherd, but this time he is smoking out a hive of bees, the same bees whose lives and care Virgil had so meticulously described in an earlier poem. At one point in the final battle, he threatens to raze the Italian citadel to the ground unless he gets a quick surrender, the same fate once suffered by his own city and its people. The fleeting moments of happiness found in the poem's first half belong in another lifetime, and Virgil is sure to have us remember this. At the funeral of a young warrior whose father had entrusted him to Aeneas' care, the hero goes to his suitcase:

> Then Aeneas brought forth two robes, stiff with gold and purple, which Sidonian Dido, delighting in the toil, had once herself with her own hands wrought for him, interweaving the web with threads of gold.

The whole second half of the poem, and in particular its famous ending, seem to question the human cost of Aeneas' mission.

More particularly, in the *Aeneid*'s second half Virgil describes the violence of a group of settlers towards an indigenous people and their ecosystem. In their desecration of the Italian landscape, the Trojans bulldoze over a wild olive tree, an *oleaster*, which, we are told, held special religious and cultural significance for the Italian community. When Aeneas' spear gets stuck in its shattered trunk, the wild olive refuses to give it up, as if protesting the Trojans' outrageous transgression. The tree comes to symbolise both the richness and frailty of indigenous customs, and, in its felling, the relentless and myopic violence of the coloniser. Virgil is also careful to point out the effects of this violence on women, and indigenous women in particular. In an earlier poem, the *Georgics*, he had compared the grieving Orpheus to a nightingale mourning the loss of her chicks, found and stolen by a 'heartless ploughman'. In the final book of the *Aeneid*, Juturna, the sister of the indigenous leader Turnus, is desperately trying to keep her brother out of harm's way. She is a river goddess, and changes her shape to that of her brother's charioteer, taking the man's place and steering Turnus out of the fiercest fighting. As in the nightingale simile, Virgil uses an image from nature to transpose one kind of love onto another:

> As when a black swallow flits through a rich lord's great mansion and wings her way through lofty halls, gleaning for her chirping nestlings tiny crumbs and scraps of food, and twitters now in the empty courts, now about the watery pools: just so Juturna is borne by the steeds through the midst of the enemy, and winging her way in the swift chariot scours all the field.

Virgil often models these similes on those he found in Homer's *Iliad* and *Odyssey*, but no Homeric precedent fits fully here. I love this one for the beauty of its central image, for the way it gets to the fierce love that sisters can have for their brothers, and for its politics. The translator uses the word 'gleaning', recalling the practice of peasant women and children who, throughout human history, have followed the harvest to save whatever scraps of grain they could, just like Ruth does in the Bible. The lines speak to what women in general, and mothers in particular, face in their efforts to survive in a rich man's world. The mansion is not a random detail.

Virgil's fictional world echoes countless real-life situations. In their book *Trees of Ireland*, Nelson and Walsh speak of the 'special place in Irish folklore' held by the native ash, venerated for reasons that are now mysterious to us; how, in an eighth-century tract of Brehon Law, the ash tree 'was classified as a "noble of the wood", *airig fedo*, with the severest penalties being exacted for damaging a tree.' Aeneas puts me in mind of Lord Mountjoy, who arrived in Ireland in the year 1600 determined to subdue the rebel Irish. He made the decision to campaign through the winter and 'clear the difficult passages', tactics which, the historian says, 'broke their hearts.'

> ... for the air being sharp, and they naked, and they being driven from their lodgings, into the woods bare of leaves, they had no shelter for themselves. Besides that, their cattle (giving them no milk in the winter) were also wasted by driving to and fro. Add that they being thus troubled in the seed time, could not sow their ground. And as in harvest time, both the deputies forces, and the garrisons, cut down their corn, before it was ripe, so now in winter time they carried away, or burnt, all the stores of victuals in secret places, whether the Rebels has conveyed them. [. . .] He had a special care to cut down and clear the difficult passages, so that our forces might with more safety meet together, and upon all occasions second one another.

Juturna and her efforts, meanwhile, make me think of Berta Cáceres (1971–2016), the Honduran activist and member of the indigenous Lenca people, assassinated for her opposition to an internationally financed mega-dam project on the Río Gualcarque in Honduras. The year before she was murdered, Cáceres was awarded the prestigious Goldman Environmental prize, and in her acceptance speech she explained the spiritual and ancestral importance of the river to the community of Río Blanco, who believe it to be inhabited and guarded by female spirits, with the river providing not just water but food and medicine to the local community.

Cáceres' life's work of political and environmental activism was based in a recognition of how different kinds of violence enable each other: violence against indigenous peoples, against nature, and against women. 'Let us wake up, humankind!' she said from the podium, 'We're out of time. We must shake our conscience free of the rapacious capitalism, racism and patriarchy that will only assure our own self-destruction'. The dam-project on the Río Gualcarque moved along well-known tracks, from the amoral decisions of international lending institutions to the nefarious influence of US imperialism in Latin America and its alliance with local elites: all those rich lords and their great mansions. Naomi Klein puts the situation in a broader context:

> . . . white Western narratives always put the apocalypse off into the future, and from an indigenous perspective, from an African perspective, from a Black perspective, in North America, apocalypses have already happened; worlds have been destroyed, cosmologies have had war waged on them, and so if we think about who should be leading these movements and whose stories we need to hear, we should hear stories from people who have lost worlds and rebuilt in the rubble.

Though he wrote long before the era of climate crisis, Virgil understands this reality; he wrote into the *Aeneid* the lost worlds and cosmologies of pre-Roman Italy. His poem helps us to remember ideas that in some parts of the world have never been forgotten, like the idea that a clean river or a healthy forest is something divine, and that their pollution and destruction is a kind of sacrilege.

*

Virgil's *Aeneid* and its afterlife make up a package-deal of influence and inspiration. Many of the most famous works of European literature drew directly on this ancient poem, and in so doing, brought a little bit of Virgil along with them. As when Dante, in his *Divine*

Comedy, makes Virgil his guide through Hell and Purgatory, in a relationship once described to me as like that between Winnie the Pooh and Christopher Robin. Virgil is a pagan, so in Dante's Christian cosmology he is not allowed into heaven. Dante looks back and Virgil is gone, just as he had been quoting Queen Dido word for word:

> I turned around and to my left—just as
> a little child, afraid or in distress,
> will hurry to his mother—anxiously,
>
> to say to Virgil: 'I am left with less
> than one drop of my blood that does not tremble:
> I recognise the signs of the old flame.'
>
> But Virgil had deprived us of himself,
> Virgil, the gentlest father, Virgil, he
> to whom I gave my self for my salvation;
>
> and even all our ancient mother lost
> was not enough to keep my cheeks, though washed
> with dew, from darkening again with tears.

Poems like the *Aeneid* and the *Divine Comedy* have often been presented to people as 'good for them' in educational and colonial situations; they have been cherished in narrow circles of power and influence. But my sense is that they have always found a wider audience of readers who, like the speakers of Latin in Chapter 1, have left little trace of their reading in the historical record.

Take Virgil's appearance in Shakespeare's most famous play, *Hamlet*. Hamlet has invited a troupe of actors to Elsinore to put on a play which, he hopes, will force a confession from his uncle. As the troupe arrives, Hamlet greets them and shares some advice, recalling a play he had once seen and liked:

> One speech in't I chiefly loved. Twas Aeneas' tale to Dido; and thereabout of it especially when he speaks of Priam's slaughter. If it live in your memory, begin at this line – let me see, let me see.

It's clear that what Hamlet is remembering is some version of *Aeneid* Book 2, yet it's equally clear that it is not Virgil's original, but rather some version or paraphrase that perhaps Shakespeare is remembering from his schooldays. I wonder what the groundlings at the Globe Theatre would have made of this moment during the first performances of the play: whether they would have been put off by a bit of insider classical knowledge or intrigued by reference to an ancient story.

The famous novel of Shakespeare's contemporary Miguel de Cervantes, *Don Quixote*, recounts the adventures of a (seemingly) mad Spanish knight and his side-kick, Sancho Panza. The novel is full of quotations from, and references to, the worlds of ancient Greece and Rome, and to Virgil in particular. There, however, the classics are competing with a whole range of other influences for the reader's attention, whether the chivalric romances of medieval Spain, or subtle hints at the Iberian peninsula's Jewish and Islamic heritage, in what for some is a two-fingers to the oppressive political climate of the time. Near the end of their adventures, Don and Sancho come upon a pair of tapestries in a roadside inn, depicting famous stories from Greece and Rome, the hero not quite cured of his delusions:

> Don Quixote noted that Helen wasn't too sorry to be stolen away, because she was laughing to herself on the sly, but the lovely Dido was shedding tears the size of walnuts. As he looked at the paintings he said: 'These two ladies were most unfortunate not to have been born in the present age, and I am even more unfortunate not to have been born in theirs; had I confronted these gentlemen, neither would Troy have been burned nor Carthage destroyed, because by my simply killing Paris all these calamities would have been

avoided.' 'I bet', said Sancho, 'that before long there won't be a single eating-house or roadside inn or hostelry or barber's shop, where there isn't a painting of the story of our deeds. But I'd like it to be done by a better artist than the one who painted these.'

In the preface to his work, Cervantes sends up the classics altogether. The author is chatting with a friend, looking for advice on how to make his new work acceptable to the right kind of audience. Just stick in a few bits of Latin, the friend advises, and you'll be taken for a scholar, proceeding to quote (and misquote) ancient Latin authors and the Bible.

Virgil was associated in his lifetime with Naples, a place with Greek origins and Oscan heritage. It is in Naples that Virgil signs his middle poem, the *Georgics*, and his ancient biography records that he lived and was buried in the city. More concrete evidence emerged relatively recently, when a carbonised fragment of papyrus from Herculaneum was read to reveal a dedication to Virgil and his friends by a local philosopher. It's in Naples that Virgil survived, not just as the famous author of the *Aeneid*, but as a kind of folk hero. In medieval times a whole series of legends circulated around the city about the poet and the magical deeds he did for its citizens: how he drove out the snakes, charmed the market to keep produce fresh, built baths to promote public health, and so on. In the classic work on the subject, first published in 1872, Domenico Comparetti put it like this:

> ... this legend originated in Naples, and thence spread into European literature – in the first instance, however, outside Italy. Its origin in Italy was entirely the work of the lower classes, and had nothing to do with poetry or literature; it was a popular superstition, founded on local records connected with Virgil's long stay in Naples and the celebrity of his tomb in that city. It was connected with certain localities, statues and monuments in the

> neighbourhood of Naples itself, to which Virgil was supposed to have given a magical power.

For me this is reminiscent of the position of St. Patrick in Irish culture: a magical patron (who also drove out the snakes) firmly based in an historical person (who, like Virgil, wrote in Latin) but who became a figure of a broad and diverse popular culture. St. Patrick's life and influence is particularly attested in place names across the island of Ireland, not unlike how Virgil's links with Naples were connected to locations in that city.

Recent scholarship has been more sceptical than Comparetti about the origin of these Virgilian legends, arguing that they came from the pens of learned scholars and travellers to the city, before passing into broader circulation. To me this would seem to miss the wood for the trees, and to underestimate the ability of a famous historical figure to live on in the folk memory of a city with which, according to the best available evidence, he was closely associated. There is a history of Naples, dating from around 1350 and written in the Neapolitan language, which preserves many of these stories, the *Cronaca di Partenope*. Some of them we know from previous literary and historical sources, but others appear for the first time, and on several occasions the author cites common opinion as their source: 'the public think that', 'the ancient Neapolitans believed', 'they believed and thought'. A few years ago, I came across one of them in Elena Ferrante's Neapolitan quartet (2012–15), four best-selling novels which tell the story of the friendship between Elena and Lila and their lives in Naples from the 1950s to the 2010s. Ferrante writes well about class, about women's lives, and about Naples itself. Like Virgil in the *Aeneid*, she is a realist, interested less in sunny visions than in what goes on. Towards the end of the final book, Lila has once again thrown Elena by announcing she is researching the history of their city, the two ever in competition. Elena wonders what she's up to, as Lila takes to telling her friend what she's discovered. She reminds Elena of the violence that marked their childhoods, and then mentions the history of San Giovanni a Carbonara, a church built on the site of a medieval dump just outside the city walls.

> In the area called Piazza di Carbonara the poet Virgil in his time ordered that every year the *ioco de Carbonara* take place, gladiator games that didn't lead to the death of men, as they did later – *morte de homini come de po è facto* (she liked that old Italian, it amused her, she quoted it to me with visible pleasure) – but gave men practice in deeds of arms: *li homini ali facti de l'arme*. Soon, however, it wasn't a matter of *ioco* or practice [. . .] Lila, between fascination and horror, spoke to me in a mixture of dialect, Italian, and very educated quotations that she had taken from who knows where and remembered by heart.

Lila, who left school at twelve, has been reading the *Cronaca di Partenope*, and has discovered not the famous poet of ancient Rome, but a local politician. In the days leading up to Bloomsday 2022, I heard ordinary Dubliners talking and joking about *Ulysses* – asking each other if they had read it, holding little events with readings and music, full of a sense of occasion that wasn't confined to the wealthy parts of town. I thought that Joyce would have been pleased to know that his famous novel, on its hundredth anniversary, was in the mouths and on the minds of the people of Dublin. It must have been the same for Virgil in medieval Naples, where the people knew and took pride in their poet, even as they joked about (not) reading his famous work.

In Ireland between the end of the seventeenth and the start of the nineteenth centuries, a large part of the population faced discrimination under the Penal Laws, which banned Catholics from holding public office, from voting, and from setting up their own schools. Faced with this discrimination, communities took education in their own hands, and a network of informal schools sprung up around the country. These were the hedge-schools, run by schoolmasters who offered instruction – for a fee – in a whole range of subjects, including, in certain cases, Latin and Greek. Schoolmasters travelled the country acting as important conduits for news and learning, sometimes even for rebellion: Cork man Micheál Óg Ó Longáin (1766–1839) is known to have carried messages for the United Irishman disguised as a poor wandering scholar. John Murphy (1753–98), a Catholic priest, spent time in the Dominican College in Seville before becoming one of the leaders of the 1798 Rebellion in county Wexford. He attended a hedge-school as a boy, and 'was said to be the equal of his teacher in Latin and Greek', a man named Martin Gunn.

Latin in general, and Virgil in particular, have long histories in Ireland, which predate the English colonisation of the island by several centuries. While the place of Latin in the hedge-schools is easily romanticised, it is based in historical evidence. Noting the scepticism of recent scholarship on the matter, Laurie O'Higgins nevertheless contends that 'eighteenth- and nineteenth-century Ireland *was* unique in Europe for significant popular study of the Classics. By "significant" I do not mean large numbers overall, but sufficient to constitute a pattern, to make a mark, and create a memory in the wider culture.' In a similar vein, Siobhán McElduff has researched the tradition of popular ballads, 'inexpensively printed and sold in Ireland from the 1700s until the middle of the twentieth century':

> These were mainly 'slip' ballads, cheaply printed on sheets of coarse paper, cut into slips, and costing a fraction of a penny. Ballad singers were omnipresent in Irish towns and at Irish fairs, sometimes to the annoyance of the authorities, especially when they ventured into

> political territory. Some, like the blind Dublin ballad singer Zozimus Moran (*c.* 1794–1846), might fall back on classical examples to defend themselves: when arrested he claimed that he was doing nothing that had not been done before by Homer and Horace.

One particular kind of ballad, known as 'hedge-school master songs' (whether or not written by hedge-school masters), McElduff notes, 'show knowledge of an enormous array of classical goddesses and heroines', from Dido and Penelope to Aurora, Flora, and Pandora (these last three popular for their rhyming potential). At a certain point in Ireland's history, then, Latin constituted what might be called an anti-colonial resource, a way for an oppressed population to maintain their dignity and intellectual independence in the face of state discrimination. This included well-educated teachers and seminarians, but it extended to a wider audience of men and women from across different social classes, who were well able to make imaginative use of the past.

As is often the case, it's a work of art that brings history to life. Brian Friel's play *Translations*, first performed in Derry's Guildhall in 1980, takes as its subject an Irish-speaking community in Donegal in 1833, as British soldiers arrive to map the area and set about translating local place names from Irish into English. The action centres on a local hedge-school, where it's Latin, Greek, and Irish that are the living languages, while English is a strange and foreign tongue. Friel's directions state that his characters' verbatim quotations from Homer, Virgil, and Ovid should be 'in no way pedantic', and much humour is drawn from how they each play with and enjoy the ancient languages. But this enjoyment is contrasted more and more with his characters' increasing desperation as their world implodes, and it is to Friel's great credit that he does not romanticise or soften that implosion. All the Homer and Virgil in the world can't, it turns out, put bread on the table, keep people in their homes, or stop the march of English across

Donegal. Suddenly the play is speaking to every society caught between empire and autonomy, between past and future, between the local and the global. In the final section of the play, Hugh the hedge-schoolmaster withdraws further and further into nostalgia, recalling to his friend their soon-abandoned adventure to join the rebels in 1798, pikes on their shoulders and the *Aeneid* in their pockets. In lines which might apply to the entire history of Latin, he gives a final lecture to his son Owen, telling him how 'it is not the literal past, the "facts" of history, that shape us, but images of the past embodied in language', and that 'we must never cease renewing those images; because once we do, we fossilise.'

*

Our final stop on this tour is perhaps the only Latin poem to rival the *Aeneid* for influence through the centuries. This is Ovid's *Metamorphoses*, written by Virgil's younger contemporary, who made his name as a love poet and suffered exile at the hands of the Roman emperor. His poem tells the history of the world as a history of the human body, full of magic and fantasy and strange transformations. The *Aeneid* 'is like a well-adorned garden', wrote Joseph Addison, the eighteenth-century journalist and editor, but in the *Metamorphoses*, 'we are walking on enchanted ground'. It's here you'll find Daedalus and Icarus and their wings of wax, King Midas and his golden touch, Ceres' frantic attempts to rescue her daughter Persephone, and Pygmalion, the man whose statue came to life. Ovid's poem, like Virgil's, tells the truth about life, once you remember that truth-telling is not necessarily equivalent to *realism*, and that fantasy can be just as useful a mode for getting at what goes on. This is something Ursula Le Guin often spoke of in relation to the marginalisation of science-fiction in the literary world of her day, so too John Berger, when he wrote that 'to separate fact and imagination ... is to stay on dry land

and never put out to sea.' For Arundhati Roy, fiction – the language of the imagination – has an ability to resist what she calls 'the sweeping simplifications of fascism':

> Hope lies in texts that can accommodate and keep alive our intricacy, our complexity, and our *density*, against the onslaught of the terrifying, sweeping simplifications of fascism. As they barrel towards us, speeding down their straight, smooth highway, we greet them with our beehive, our maze. We keep our complicated world, with all its seams exposed, alive in our writing.

You could perhaps say the same about any successful work of art, and for me Roy's words hold true for both the *Aeneid* and the *Metamorphoses*, though others may disagree.

Readers have always found in Ovid's poem something liberating: in its complex depiction of human gender and sexuality, in its drawing together of the animal and human worlds, in its folktale structure, and in the credence it gives to magical realities. At the end of his poem, Ovid gives pride of place to the vegetarian philosopher-priest Pythagoras (of the famous theorem), who chants about reincarnation and eternal recurrence, the whole universe in flux and each of us different today than we were yesterday, or will be tomorrow. It's a profoundly radical poem, and coming from some of the other Latin classics, it can seem like a breath of fresh air. Yet the *Metamorphoses* shares something with Terence's *The Mother-in-Law*, in that its world is often nightmarish and uncomfortable. This is a poem which features not one but two world-destroying floods; a poem where Mother Earth is reduced to pleading with the Sun to stop the baking of the planet's surface before everything turns to dust. The *Metamorphoses* features a huge amount of sexual violence, most of it directed against women. *Da ne femina sim*, prays Caenis, after being raped by the god Neptune: 'make me not a woman'. As with Terence's play, there is little out-of-date in the poem's depiction of this kind of violence, and the shocking nature of some of its stories does not make them any less true-to-life.

Women feature again and again in the *Metamorphoses* as weavers and storytellers, one practice connected to the other. Ovid imagines his entire poem as a kind of tapestry, spun out like you might spin out wool into thread. The poem's most famous weaver appears in Book 6. This is Arachne, the low-born prodigy whose awesome skill provokes the wrath of Minerva herself. Challenged by Minerva to a weaving contest, Arachne's effort is so beautiful that the goddess cannot handle being bested by this unashamed mortal. So she destroys Arachne, and then turns her into a spider, forced to weave her webs for the rest of time. I think that Ovid has something in common with Karl Marx here, in that he recognises that before labour is something by which to earn a living, or something manipulated by the powers that be (a vengeful heaven in one case, a system of capitalist production in the other), it is first and foremost this amazing thing that human beings do, transforming raw materials into objects both beautiful and useful, adding value through effort and imagination. Arachne is a peasant who challenges a goddess, she is self-made and fearless, and so an inherent threat to authority. So fine is her work, Ovid says, that you would think her depictions were the real thing. And the poet is keenly aware, here and throughout his poem, of what unites the artist and the artisan, a relationship evidenced by the fact that the word 'poetry' comes from the Greek verb meaning to make or do. Arachne makes her tapestry, but Ovid makes Arachne.

Latin poetry is full of spinners and weavers, from the woman who 'adds a night-shift to her day's work', weaving by firelight to keep her husband and children clothed (Virgil, *Aeneid* 8), to the magical Fates, who spin the yarns that represent individual human lives, and sing the future (Catullus, poem 64). As in Claudia's epitaph, discussed in Chapter 1, this is not simply a stereotypical and reductive depiction of women's lives. It speaks to the value of made things through time, of artisans and their inherently creative work. Dublin, the city where I live, has its own history of weavers, 'cotton, silk, woollen and linen weavers, concentrated in the overcrowded Coombe and Earl of Meath's Liberty, the city's "largest occupational group" at the end of the eighteenth century, working mainly from their homes and in poor conditions.' Today, in my part of the world, clothes mostly come from elsewhere, made as cheaply as possible and with little regard for the welfare or working conditions of the spinners and weavers of Bangladesh and Vietnam. In my part of the world, words like *warp* and *weft* and *loom* are fading from memory. One role that the arts fulfil, perhaps, is in the fight against this loss of memory, and the authority that loss of memory gives to the status quo. History is there to contextualise the present, to remind us that things were different once, and so could be different again. Remembering the weavers, ancient and modern, their work and their struggles to survive, becomes an act of co-ordination, grounding us more fully in the world.

Together, Virgil and Ovid gave to later times a story which has been retold over and over again. This is the tale of Orpheus and Eurydice, known in different versions in ancient Greek literature, but most famous for its appearance in the two Roman poets. Orpheus is an outstanding musician, able to charm nature and the animals with his song. His wife, Eurydice, dies from a snakebite and, unwilling to endure this loss, Orpheus travels to the Underworld to retrieve her. His music earns the respect of the gods – and free-passage to retrieve his wife – on one condition: that he doesn't look at Eurydice until they have reached the world above. But Orpheus looks back, and Eurydice is lost again and forever, the hero then wandering in a frozen wilderness until he is beaten to death by a group of women. Myths from ancient Greece and Rome have never lost their appeal, and this is one of many. This one says something in a particularly concentrated way about love and death, about the power of art, and about the necessity of moving on, however difficult that may be. You'll find Orpheus on the walls of medieval cathedrals and at the birth of modern opera (Monteverdi's *L'Orfeo*), in twentieth-century cinema (*Orphée*, *Black Orpheus*), in modern pop music (Arcade Fire's *Reflektor*, Hozier's 'Talk', from *Wasteland, Baby!*) and musical theatre (*Hadestown*). Writing about *La casa sin sosiego* ('*The House Without Calm*'), an opera first performed in Buenos Aires in 1991, Lía Galán sums up the myth's history as 'a popular fable of all times to express love which defies death.' Eurydice is now Teresa, a disappeared victim of Argentina's military and civil dictatorship (1976–83), and Orpheus is Juan, her husband desperate for information.

What gives the myth its potency is that, to steal a line from Eavan Boland ('The Pomegranate'), you can enter it anywhere. As Orpheus, as Eurydice, as both together, as a neutral observer. Margaret Atwood ('Orpheus (1)') brings out the arrogance implicit in Orpheus' wish, which subjects his wife to a second death, so final in Virgil's version:

> 'What madness, Orpheus, what dreadful madness has brought disaster alike upon you and me, poor soul? See, again the cruel Fates call me back, and sleep seals my swimming eyes. And now farewell!

Ovid is more forgiving, allowing Orpheus and Eurydice a happy reunion in the underworld, as is Boland, who nevertheless retells the loss from Eurydice's point of view ('Eurydice Speaks'). Ovid, it should also be noted, follows a thread found in earlier Greek versions, which tells of Orpheus' bisexuality. Seamus Heaney sets his version on the London Underground ('The Underground'), capturing the violence implied in Orpheus' pursuit yet ultimately emphasising his humane naivety, a new husband on honeymoon. Czesław Miłosz, writing, as Peter Sirr notes, at the very end of his life, has a version suffused with calm sadness, and an unrivalled description of Orpheus' song, with its gorgeous litany of life on earth.

The myth, then, is as various as its readers: a story of true love, male arrogance, the power of art, all those things and more. Céline Sciamma's 2019 film *Portrait of a Lady on Fire* captures the appeal and versatility of the myth well. Two women are staying together on a remote island, their only companion a young maid who gradually befriends them. One evening the three sit round as one reads from Ovid's version in French translation. The camera moves between the three faces as they register the twists and turns of the story. At the end, there is disagreement: did Orpheus do the right thing or not? 'He doesn't make the lover's choice, but the poet's', comes the reply. This scene for me speaks to the best of the tradition I've been describing in this chapter, the tradition of the Latin classics, in the way it forms one link in a long chain of reimagination and reinvention. A good story is pliable, it can be reshaped and remoulded according to different concerns and different points of view. Ovid has inspired countless works of literature and fine art, no less than Virgil. The work of both constitutes a democratic archive of human creativity which, though often exclusive in formal educational terms, nevertheless has always reached a wider audience. Virgil and Ovid means Shakespeare and Cervantes and Titian and Rembrandt and many more, but also the streets of medieval Naples and the hedge-schools of eighteenth-century Ireland, filtered back through the work of Elena Ferrante and Brian Friel. It means someone who sees a film or a show and is prompted to think about old tales from ancient Rome. All of this is part of the story. The best classics, of any kind, are never pretentious, though they can be made so. They say what most of us can't say about the world and our lives in it.

The stories recounted here give full humanity to slaves and critique the hypocrisies of a slave-owning society. They recognise the unique and life-giving value of the natural world and its fragility in the face of human greed and warfare, as well as the importance of artisans and their creative and productive work. They shine a light on the worst aspects of human behaviour, including colonial and sexual violence. If capitalism, the economic system under which most of us live, achieves its goal of profit-at-all-costs by trying to disconnect us from each other, from our common past, and from the world around us; if it commodifies people as being of greater or lesser value depending on their race, their gender, their class, or their productivity; if it would prefer us to buy rather than to make or repair, and to forget the horrors of war, then there is something anti-capitalist about these works of art. They connect us to the human chain that runs from those cave paintings in Altamira and Lascaux through to street parties and festivals around the world today.

3

Latin to Romance

What happened to Latin after the Roman empire? Two things. First, it remained a language of education and culture in Europe throughout the Middle Ages, gradually fossilising into a system of rules based on the classical literature of ancient Rome. This is the Latin that many people in Ireland learnt up until the end of the 1970s – when you still needed a pass in Latin to get into university – and in fewer numbers since. To call this language a dead language is only partly correct. Certainly, it is not a living language in the sense I talked about in Chapter 1: you don't use Latin to speak with others in daily life. Yet as many students of the language will tell you, the Latin archive is extraordinarily rich, containing as if by magic the remnants of human lives and human experience. To dismiss it simplistically as a 'dead' language is to side with what G. K. Chesterton once called 'the arrogant oligarchy of those who merely happen to be walking about', and to ignore the deep connection between the living and the dead which has been so central to human communities through time. ('Only a uniquely modern form of egotism', wrote John Berger, has broken this interdependence: the Roman poet Horace would agree.) Second, Latin, as most people know, turned into a series of modern languages known as the Romance languages, including French, Spanish, Portuguese, Italian, Romanian and a whole host of smaller languages, now spoken by millions of people around the world. But the exact relationship between these two kinds of Latin – living and dead – can be a little unclear. In this final chapter, I'm going to explore Latin's journey to Romance.

My experience in first learning Latin was one of curiosity and puzzlement. I can still remember being struck by my teacher's translation of a half-line from Virgil's *Aeneid*, and feeling the pull of poetry as many people do in secondary school. Aeneas is about to tell Dido the story of the fall of the Troy, but it's late in the night and 'the falling stars are counselling sleep'. Aeneas thinks it's time for bed, but Dido is eager to hear about her guest's adventures, so they stay up, and he tells the story of the wooden horse and the destruction of the city. But in order to translate this poetry – and for many of us, myself included, there was more guesswork than we would have liked to admit – I had to study the system of rules and endings that make up Latin grammar. Tables of nouns and verbs, recited and learnt off as best you could, in a kind of chant that is familiar to many students of Latin. *Amo, amas, amat* ('I love, 'you love', 'he/she/it loves'), pronounced in our normal accents, and with the stress always on the final syllable, the bit that changes. It was only years later that I copped how artificial this system was, that the stress of a two-syllabled Latin word is always on the first syllable; how little we had tried to bring our Dublin vowels in line with something approaching modern Italian, one of Latin's modern descendants. The vividness of the poetry was in stark contrast to the artificiality of the grammar. There seemed to be little connection between this language and any modern language I knew, and the idea that Latin was the ancestor of the Romance languages seemed irrelevant.

In my study of the language since, I've been retraining myself to appreciate Latin as a living language. One step on this journey was coming across some ancient language-learning textbooks that have been recently edited by Eleanor Dickey. These are short and simple dialogues that originate in the Roman empire from some point between the second and fourth centuries CE, meant for those who had to learn Latin as a foreign language. Crucially, these language learners were learning a living language, which they needed to acquire for practical reasons: a business trip perhaps, or a new job. In their listing of simple everyday activities, they remind me of holiday phrasebooks before the internet, when you need to order a coffee or find a doctor in a foreign language, and of Irish class in primary school, when we used to read out our morning routine. 'When I get up in the morning I put on my clothes, I brush my teeth, I eat my breakfast', and so on. Or, as one of these Latin dialogues begins: 'Before dawn, I woke up from sleep; I got up from bed; I sat down.' Another features a short conversation between two friends, going to check up on a mutual friend of theirs, Lucius, who has been sick. *Ubi manet?* the first friend asks the second: where is he staying? When I first tried to translate this simple text, I was puzzled because I had only ever met the verb *manēre* in formal contexts; the dictionary definition I had learnt in school was 'to wait' or 'to remain'. Something that armies and emotions do, not ordinary people. So it was a small and disruptive revelation to come across the verb in a fragment of real-life conversation, where – of course – the meaning you need is 'stay'. Here was Latin as a living language.

It is useful, then, to think of the history of Latin after the Roman empire in terms of two branches, one 'high' and the other 'low'; a high language of culture, literature, religion, and education, and a low language of everyday life. The distinction is mostly accurate, as long as you remember that the two branches are not sealed off from each other, and indeed they often blur together. Poets and educators and priests used ordinary spoken language in their daily lives, and people would have had access to, and would have been able to appreciate in certain contexts, the language of high culture. If you know something of European choral and liturgical music, you'll have a sense of how Latin is something people have valued in their lives across many centuries. What's confusing is that the names change. The high branch keeps the name 'Latin' but the low branch fractures into several different languages, each under a different name. The key point, though, is that they are different parts of the same thing. Latin is a continuum that stretches from the time of the ancient Romans up to the present day, handed down by word of mouth from parents to children over thousands of years, the truest aspect of its human chain. To ask whether Latin is a living or dead language is, in many ways, to ask the wrong question. It is both of those things, and to understand how this is the case, I'd like to share with you the arguments of Roger Wright, who has worked on this subject for many years.

*

Imagine yourself in a town somewhere in modern France or Spain in the year 400 CE. What languages are the people around you speaking? Very probably there is more than one language being spoken, and each of them sounds subtly different in the mouth of each speaker you hear. Of the Latin speakers, some of them are well-to-do and highly educated, able not just to speak 'good' Latin but to write it correctly too; they are familiar with the works of Caesar and Cicero and can write just like them, though their spoken language is a little different to the one those ancient Romans would have recognised, because all languages change and develop across time and space. Some of the people you hear around you will not have had any formal education at all, and many will not be able to read and write, but nevertheless can speak with their well-to-do compatriots on equal terms. For much of its life in the Roman empire (traditionally taken to end in western Europe in 476 CE) and the centuries immediately following, Latin comprised one, very diverse, linguistic world. As outlined in Chapter 1, the language would have varied from place to place and from person to person, according to context and the identities and moods of its speakers. It was considerably more diverse than it appears in surviving written evidence, because written language is by nature a conservative and often inaccurate representation of its spoken counterpart.

This language kept growing more and more diverse over time, a process that has continued into the present day. If you wanted to, you could refer to all the Romance languages as modern Latin, though the differences between them have grown so large that a speaker of one of them will not necessarily understand a speaker of another, and so it's practical to call them by different names. That this name change should have occurred in the first place is a matter of political and social history. For Wright, the key transition begins at the court of the emperor Charlemagne, based at Aachen in western Germany, either side of the year 800 CE, and is largely complete by the twelfth century, by which time the new Romance languages were no longer synonymous with Latin. Charlemagne saw his power as a direct inheritance of the Roman empire, and the scholars of his court set about trying – with much success – to revive the cultural legacies of that empire. Many important manuscripts, for instance, which ensured the survival of Roman authors into the modern world, date not from ancient Rome but from this time and place. One aspect of this revival, or *renovatio*, was an attempt to improve standards of Latin in general, and to recreate the glory days of Caesar, Cicero, and the famous poets (the history of Latin is full of such 'classicising' moments, when people are inspired to 'get back' to an imagined and noble past). For the scholars at court, proper or good Latin meant the language of ancient Rome, not the language they spoke and heard in the street. By this time, however, the everyday language was diverging more and more from its narrow, 'classical', counterpart.

Amongst the most influential scholars at Charlemagne's court was Alcuin of York (*c.* 735–804) who, as his name suggests, was raised in a place where Latin was learnt as second language, rather than as a learned version of one's native language, as it was for many of those in continental western Europe. His concern was to have Latin taught as he had learned it, with every letter pronounced individually, rather than, as in every living language, a transcription of sounds people knew first from spoken language. An academic idea of Latin was preferred to its spoken reality. To use an example of Wright's, think of the difference between *chante* (he/she sings) and *chantent* (they sing) in modern French. A native speaker knows from experience that these words are pronounced the same, despite being written differently. If you learnt them on your own and as a second language, however, you might reasonably pronounce both syllables in *chantent*. What's interesting is that these two strands continue today. Latin learners in English-speaking countries usually adopt our best guess at what ancient 'classical' pronunciation was like, yet make little or no concession to Romance sounds in their pronunciation of Latin. Latin learners in modern Italy, to the best of my knowledge, happily bring their native sounds into the pronunciation of the language, with (to my mind) more attractive results.

A very influential section of society, at a particular point in European history, deliberately separated out the high and low branches of the language. This was partly an idealising attempt to enforce classical standards of writing and speech (as when someone today bemoans bad grammar), and partly a necessity. The political and religious elite of western Europe needed to be understood, especially in matters of law and religion, and to be understood you need to speak to people in ways they can understand. At the Council of Tours in 813, it was decreed that sermons should be given in the *rustica romana lingua*, 'the peasant Roman tongue', that is, in language that the congregation could understand. The first generally accepted written evidence for the Romance languages, meanwhile, comes from the following decades, in similar cases where understanding was at a premium: a military pact known as the Oaths of Strasbourg, dated to 14 February 842, and some legal oaths relating to land in southern Italy (the 'Placiti Cassinesi'), an area beyond Carolingian control, dated 960–3. From here on in, as will be explored below, the two branches of Latin go their separate ways, though remember that this distinction is, at least in the beginning, artificial and political. It was implemented and enforced in the areas where Charlemagne's power and that of his successors held sway, and in time came to be accepted across Europe. This picture of the situation is necessarily general, and there is so much that cannot be known about how people considered their relationship to Latin over such a long period of time. But if you accept the argument, then one big conclusion follows: that the language most people know today as Latin – the 'dead' language of learning, religion, and culture – was a creation, not of ancient Rome, but of the scholars and intellectuals of medieval Europe.

*

Let's now trace Latin's 'high' branch though the medieval period. There is no neat chronological journey from 'early' to 'late' to 'medieval' Latin. Words and constructions which appear in Plautus (around 200 BCE) are also found in the modern Romance languages, while many writers in the medieval and early modern periods were able to write intricate Latin prose that Cicero himself (the famous orator, first century BCE) would have appreciated. It's not a question of when someone is writing, that is, but of how they are writing. Remember that our evidence is restricted to written sources, and that the medieval Latin archive is heavily weighted in favour of Christian sources written by educated people in privileged positions. Christianity brought its own worldview to the language, greatly influenced by the Bible in its Hebrew, Greek, and Latin versions, as new words appeared and old ones found new meanings. *Christus* comes from Greek and *amen* comes from Hebrew, while words like *episcopus* ('overseer') and *peccare* ('to make a mistake') took on radically new meanings. Medieval written sources in Latin vary hugely in style and tone and content across hundreds of years; they include both non-Christian and non-elite writing. Between the final decades of the Roman empire in the west (*c.* 400 CE) and the twelfth century, when the Latin/Romance distinction took root in earnest, Latin was one big system of expression, which we can glimpse at several different moments in time.

Take, firstly, the *Confessions* of St. Augustine (354–430). Augustine was a north African bishop, educated at Carthage, Rome, and Milan, whose writings would exert a profound influence on all subsequent Christian theology. He could write and speak in the best Latin of his day, and lots of his writing survives. But his most famous work is his most unorthodox, an autobiography written between 397 and 400 CE, and seemingly to himself. From my limited acquaintance with the work, it's by turns fascinating and difficult, as you feel yourself able to relate to his personal struggles yet at sea in a strange world of deeply serious and penitent religious belief:

> Great are you, O Lord, and surpassingly worthy of praise. Great is your goodness, and your wisdom is incalculable. And humanity, which is but a part of your creation, wants to praise you; even though humanity bears everywhere its own mortality, and bears everywhere the evidence of its own sin and the evidence that you resist the proud. And even so humanity, which is but a part of your creation, longs to praise you. You inspire us to take delight in praising you, for you have made us for yourself, and our hearts are restless until they rest in you.

This is writing that Cicero would have found very strange indeed, not least because of its interiority, biblical quotations, and Christian ideas. Augustine is writing a kind of Latin that no one had written before, far from any non-Christian classical model, with an immediacy that has always appealed to readers. He is writing before the end of the Roman empire, yet in a completely new way. 'There have been various attempts to find precedents for this form of opening', writes James O'Donnell, 'but in the history of Latin literature, its originality and oddity are clear.'

By contrast, move now to the high medieval period, and the Norman invasion of Ireland in the twelfth century. An extremely well-educated priest and diplomat, known to history as Gerald of Wales (*c.* 1146–1223), spent just over two years in Ireland between 1183 and 1186, and wrote two works about the island and its people. These works are disparaging about the native Irish, and deeply colonial: Ireland is a desolate, impassable, and rainy place, the kind of language that colonisers have always used when claiming that a *terra nullius*, a 'nobody's land', is rightfully theirs; its people 'live like beasts'. Gerald writes in impeccable classical Latin, the kind which, in contrast to Augustine's *Confessions*, Cicero would have recognised as modelled on his own.

> When I consider how short and changeable is the life we lead, what seems to me quite excellent is the plan of those who, their life's road not yet ended, thought it worth their time and effort to leave some outstanding earthly memorial behind them, to make their fame last, and to live on, at least in memory, after this fleeting existence ...

This opening is full of the elaborate, well-balanced phrases and studied self-effacement (not to mention outstanding self-confidence) which you find at the beginning of so many classical works. This particular style, with its long and winding sentences, was made famous by Cicero and the historian Livy, in contrast to the very different style of other Latin prose writers like Sallust and Tacitus. But over time it was the Ciceronian and Livian standard that became the model, and there is nothing here that would have been out of place in late first-century BCE Rome, despite the fact that Gerald is writing in twelfth-century Wales.

There is a great deal of medieval Latin that I pass over here, including much theology and science and religious material, the mainstream of Christian European thought. Instead I'd like to show you something from the margins of this world, a poem discovered in a manuscript in the Bodleian Library in Oxford by the scholar Peter Dronke, only in the 1960s. It's a mysterious ballad-poem, originating in northern Italy in the tenth century and recorded in a manuscript copied at Fleury in the Loire Valley sometime after the year 1000. It's not explicitly a religious text, though it seems to draw on a range of classical and religious influences: the poetry of Ovid, the *Song of Songs*, and popular ballad traditions. It's called *Foebus Abierat*, or 'Phoebus was gone', referring to the Sun-God of ancient Rome, but spelt with that characteristic Italian *f* over the Greek and Latin *ph*. A woman is visited by the ghost of her lover on a moonlit night: the narrator is overcome, and when the ghost departs, she melts away in floods of tears. A translation of the poem by Irish poet Eavan Boland (1944–2020) is available online, of which I give the first two stanzas here:

> Phoebus was gone, all gone, his journey over.
> His sister was riding high: nothing bridled her.
> Her light was falling, shining into woods and rivers.
> Wild animals opened their jaws wide, stirred to prey.
> But in the human world all was sleep, pause, relaxation, torpor.
>
> One night, in an April which had just gone by,
> The likeness of my love stood beside me suddenly.

He called my name so quietly. He touched me gently.
His voice was drowning in tears. It failed completely.
His sighs overwhelmed him. Finally, he could not speak clearly.

Boland refers to the poem as a 'dream vision', and reproduces its hypnotic rhyming structure in her translation. It is 'rapid, passionate; a quick arc of sounds and meaning done in a language which does not usually bend to speed'; 'the long-ago cry of a woman finding and losing a body and soul.' She showcases a text which sits somewhere between the high and low branches of Latin I've been discussing: the work of a literate and skilful poet, yet in tune with a world of romance, desire, and popular culture far removed from many standard pictures of medieval life. She repeats a point made by Jane Stevenson: though the author of the poem remains anonymous, there is no reason why it could not have been a woman, perhaps a woman in religious life.

*

The evidence for 'low' Latin is harder to find in the early medieval period, though it does exist. By 'low' Latin I mean written evidence for spoken language and texts that were meant for a general, rather than an elite audience, at a time when Latin was still one big, diverse, language. One example is that of Egeria's travel diary, discussed in Chapter 1. Another is the Old Latin gospels, the ones revised by St. Jerome at the end of the fourth century CE, meant to be read and understood by wider Christian communities, not just the religious elite. In his study of their language, Philip Burton has tentatively identified changes which seem to have occured in Latin by the time the gospels were translated into the language, as well as moments when the translators are being conservative and perhaps resisting new words in favour of older ones. The language of these gospel texts is full of the influence of Greek and features plenty of constructions that are familiar from the classical langauge, but it is equally full of simple and straightforward narratives in an unadorned literary style. When Jesus feeds the five thousand (Matthew 14:16), he tells the disciples to give the people something to eat: the word for 'eat' is not the classical *edere* but rather *manducare*, the same verb that the emperor Augustus used in that private letter, and the same verb that will come into French (*manger*) and Italian (*mangiare*). This suggests that it must have had a currency in everyday language. Sometimes two competing variants are used with equal frequency, like *ire* and *vadere* for 'to go', and sometimes changes that will occur later are not found. In the Old Latin gospels *sapere* has not yet replaced *scire* as the standard verb for 'to know', while 'to buy' is still *emere* rather than *comparare* (like Spanish, *comprar*), and a house is still a *domus* and not yet a *casa*.

Now fast forward to the first half of the seventh century CE. In what is now Spain, the political consensus known as the Roman empire has broken down, but life goes on, and there is a legal system operating to settle disputes. Someone has scratched a declaration about witnesses with a sharp object onto a piece of slate; this slate is one of 150 or so which have been discovered in the area between Ávila and the Portuguese border in the Spanish province of Castile and León. Here is some of what it says:

> While I was in the house of Desiderius, there came along Froila and he said to me: 'Up you get, clerk, and let us go to the house of Busa and Fastenus'. It transpired we went to the house of Busa.

This slate documents language (and literacy) as a means of getting access to mediation, resolution, judgement. We are at a moment in the history of the language when substantial changes are taking place, and modern Spanish is coming into being. This seemingly mundane text is full of what Adams calls 'proto-Spanish features.' In the first phrase above the verb *stare*, 'to stand', is being used in place of *esse*, 'to be', in a way that anticipates the same shared duties of *estar* and *ser* in modern Spanish, where *estar* is used of transitory states ('I'm in the cinema') and *ser* for those that are more permanent ('I'm your friend'). *Esse* also appears to be filling in for the past tense of the verb *vadere*, 'to go' (in the phrase, 'we went to the house of Busa'), again in a way exactly parallel to modern Spanish.

Like any language, Latin was and is constantly changing, and there is no one moment when Latin became Romance. This is highlighted by one of the most interesting pieces of evidence I've come across in relation to the development of the Romance languages, a piece of graffiti etched on the wall of a Roman catacomb sometime around the year 800 CE. A decree had recently been issued in the city that the holy liturgy should be said, not aloud, but under one's breath, and someone took the opportunity to scratch a reminder on the wall. 'Don't say the mysteries out loud', it says, or, in the original:

Non dicere ille secrita a bboce

Here is a tiny glimpse of a language somewhere between Latin and Romance. Someone else has come along later and added the second *b* in *bboce* (like Italian *voce*), someone who felt one letter didn't transcribe accurately enough the spoken sound. As Petrucci notes, there are things here which anticipate directly the dialects of central and southern Italy – where in certain places *dicere* is still the word 'to say', rather than the standard Italian form *dire* – and the Italian language, where the Latin word for 'that' (*ille*) has become one of the words for 'the'. At the same time, then, that Alcuin and the scholars of Charlemagne's court were embarking on their quest to return to ancient Rome, and at the same time, too, that monks somewhere in Ireland or Britain were creating one of the most famous examples of high Latin religious culture – the illuminated gospels known as the Book of Kells – priests were gathering beneath the city of Rome and speaking a language arguably closer to modern Italian than ancient Latin. The context is still a religious one, but the graffito speaks to the world of ordinary Romans in which these priests would have lived, and a language almost completely unrecorded in the historical archive, except for small and special moments like this one.

*

As the centuries went on, Latin as a language of power, authority, and learning increasingly lost out to vernacular languages all over Europe. The bitter disputes of the Reformation in the sixteenth century were in part a dispute over whether the word of God should remain in Latin or be translated into languages people spoke in their daily lives. The 'dead' language, or Latin's high branch, began an enforced retreat from the central position it had occupied in the medieval period. Nevertheless, all over Europe, it remained – right through the fifteenth, sixteenth, and seventeenth centuries – a language of kings and princes and those who moved in their circles. Across the continent there are buildings and monuments and museums and churches on which you can still see Latin today. Not only that, it remained the language of international politics, diplomacy, and scholarship, a kind of intellectual lingua franca for Europe's elite political and intellectual classes. In the 1560s Queen Elizabeth I of England was presented with a phrasebook by Sir Christopher Nugent (*c.* 1544–1602), now preserved in the Benjamin Iveagh Library at Farmleigh House in Dublin. It's eighteen pages long, and in three distinct hands it lists phrases in Irish, Latin, and English side by side. *Conas atá tú* becomes *Quomodo habes*, which in turn becomes *How doe you?*; *Táim go maith* goes to *Bene sum* then *I am well*, and so on down the page, the three languages equal partners. Elizabeth was an excellent linguist, whose Latin translation of the historian Tacitus has recently been rediscovered; Latin is the language in which, so the story goes, she conversed with Grace O'Malley, her

Irish counterpart and rival, in a famous meeting between the two women. Elizabeth, of course, was not just a linguist but a colonising monarch, whose agents in Dublin Castle were in this same decade writing back and forth to each other in Latin.

Scholars often refer to this twilight period of the high language as 'Neo-Latin', which can apply to anything from sixteenth-century poetry to the Latin decrees of the Vatican into the present day. As David Butterfield has written, this long period is marked by 'purification and decline', as Latin becomes more and more the language of ever smaller and more privileged sections of society, having by now lost any real connection to daily life and spoken language, though it will hold its place in education right up until the twentieth century. Just as at the court of Charlemagne in the ninth century, there is more and more a retreat to narrow and idealised forms of poetry and prose, with conscious imitation of classical models the most prized form of expression. Nevertheless, it's important to remember that even in this limited state, Latin could still be a vehicle for humane and sometimes radical work. The seventeenth century is the age when the last Latin masterpieces were composed, not in poetry, but in early modern science. René Descartes (1591–1650) was doubting everything in order to get back to first principles, the only thing he was sure of his own consciousness: 'I think, therefore I am', he wrote, *cogito ergo sum*. Johannes Kepler (1571–1630) and Isaac Newton (1642–1727), meanwhile, laid the foundations of modern physics, with the latter's *Philosophiae Naturalis Principia Mathematica* ('Mathematical Principles of Natural Philosophy') published in Latin in 1687.

In the seventeenth century, 'science' had a much wider definition than it does today, incorporating not just what we think of as the sciences but also philosophy and theology, metaphysics and astronomy. Nor did Latin have a complete monopoly on scientific publication: it was a way to get your work to the best in the field, but if you wanted to be understood by a general audience, the vernacular was increasingly the way to go. This holds true for the work of Galileo Galilei (1564–1642), whose *Starry Messenger* (*Sidereus Nuncius*, 1610) showcased his observations of the night sky, the lunar surface, and the moons of Jupiter through a new and exciting piece of technology: the telescope. Online you can find scans of the first edition of this book, which includes fine drawings of the lunar surface and the constellations. But Galileo was equally famous as a stylist in the Italian language, and it was his *Dialogue on the Two Great World Systems*, published in Italian in 1632, that provoked the Vatican. In this work Galileo shared his increasing conviction that Copernicus was right in his belief about a heliocentric universe; he was summoned to Rome in 1633 and sentenced to house arrest, where he remained until his death in 1642. His *Dialogue*, though written in Italian, adopts the literary form of Plato and Cicero, and combines beautiful writing with cutting-edge science. At the end of the first day's discussion, one of the speakers marvels at human ingenuity: the poets and the architects, the musicians, artists, and navigators. Most of all, though, Sagredo is impressed with whoever it was who came up with human language, the one who:

> . . . dreamed of finding the means to communicate his deepest thoughts to any other person, though distant by mighty intervals of time and place! Of talking with those who are in India; of speaking to those who are not yet born and will not be born for a thousand or ten thousand years; and with what facility, by the different arrangements of twenty characters upon a page.

Sagredo could be summing up the history of Latin.

In the same year that Galileo published his *Dialogue*, Bento Spinoza (1632–77) was born in Amsterdam. Expelled from his Jewish community as a young man for what were considered dangerously atheistic beliefs, Spinoza made his living as a lens grinder (*opticus insignis*, 'an outstanding optician', his friend Leibniz called him), and also kept a sketchbook, now lost, but reimagined in *Bento's Sketchbook* by John Berger. He learnt Latin in his twenties at the school of a man called Francis Van den Enden, an ex-Jesuit later executed in Paris for his alleged involvement in a plot against Louis XIV; we know that Van den Enden directed his pupils in the plays of Terence, put on for the citizens of Amsterdam, in the years 1657 and 1658, with Spinoza in the cast. This education stayed with the young philosopher, and throughout his works scholars have traced quotations from Ovid, Tacitus, and especially Terence. In his *Theological-Political Treatise* of 1670, Spinoza argued for a rationalist and historical understanding of the Bible (kick-starting modern biblical criticism in the process) and a democratic idea of the state in which far-reaching tolerance and freedom of expression were the orders of the day.

> It very clearly follows from the fundamental principles of the state which I explained above that its ultimate purpose is not to dominate or control people by fear or subject them to the authority of another. On the contrary, its aim is to free everyone from fear so that they may live in security as far as possible, that is, so that they may retain, to the highest possible degree, their natural right to live and act without harm to themselves or to others. It is not, I contend, the purpose of the state to turn people from rational beings into beasts or automata, but rather to allow their minds and bodies to develop in their own ways in security and enjoy the free use of reason, and not to participate in conflicts based on hatred, anger, or deceit or in malicious disputes with each other. Therefore, the true purpose of the state is in fact freedom.

In the last years of his life, amidst an increasingly deteriorating political situation in Amsterdam, Spinoza was quietly working on his

Ethics, a five-book treatise on how to live, composed as a series of propositions and proofs in the manner of Euclid and the classics of medieval philosophy. While the form may have been traditional, the content was anything but, as the *Ethics* argues that our human minds and human bodies are integral parts of the same whole, not separate and distinct (as Descartes had held), and that God and Nature are, controversially and mysteriously, the same thing.

Latin has been very often throughout its life a language of centralised and domineering authority, from the decrees of Roman emperors to the bulls of the Papacy. But Galileo and Spinoza show us a language of free, creative, and progressive thinking. In certain ways the two men are quite different characters ('what does philosophy have to do with measuring anything?' Galileo once said), but they shared a willingness to be puzzled, a belief in the power of human understanding, and a certain bravery in having the courage of their convictions. For Galileo, Spinoza, and indeed for Spinoza's teacher Van den Enden, there was nothing fusty about Latin: it was razor-sharp.

*

Let's go back now to our low branch, the spoken language, where we left it in the catacombs beneath the city of Rome. This language continues to develop in a mostly unhistorical way, by which I mean that there is little written evidence, understandably enough, for all the daily conversations of Latin speakers over hundreds of years. It's a hidden history, which we can glimpse from two different angles. First, from the perspective of those scholars and teachers who are concerned about bad grammar, and people not writing their Latin properly. Already by the end of the third century, in a text copied at Bobbio in northern Italy sometime in the seventh century, someone made up a list of corrections: that it's *rivus*, not *rius* (for 'river'), *mensa*, not *mesa* (for 'table'), *auris*, not *oricla* (for 'ear'), and so on. Spoken language is moving further and further away from a written standard, which is in turn disrupting that written standard. Second, we have the evidence before our ears, the words that have come into Romance as a result of decisions (if that's the right word) made in different parts of Europe over hundreds of years, by many diverse speech communities. In many areas they ditched *cras* ('tomorrow') and used a version of *mane* ('in the morning') to give us *demain*, *domani*, and *mañana*; they replaced the Latin *loqui* ('to speak') with a whole host of more colourful verbs related to the telling of a story (*narrare*, *fabulari*, *parabolare*), and they took in words from the languages and cultures they interacted with: *guerre* for 'war' from the Germans, *caminare* for 'walk' from the Gauls, and *algodón* for 'cotton' from the Arabs of Andalusia. Language not as a scholarly standard but a living ecosystem, still with us today.

Only very gradually, over many centuries, did these spoken versions of Latin enter into the worlds of history and literature, traditionally defined. Dante, for example, not only chose his native dialect for his *Comedy*, but also wrote a treatise in Latin in which he explored the different varieties of the spoken language in his day. 'Romance' meant originally 'Roman', and to speak Romance was to speak in a Roman way. That label came to be used by those who wanted to distinguish between elite and non-elite language, 'Latin' and 'Romance' respectively, in the areas where Charlemagne and his successors held power, but it was also used in the rich literary traditions of medieval France, when a *romanz* came to mean a story of epic adventure and true love – life as you might read it in a book – and so giving the most common modern meaning of the word. If history were written differently, Romance might be the mainstream, with Latin its tributary: the distinction is an artificial one for varieties of the same thing, and literature was not simply the concern of one rather than the other.

Even still, the living language – speaking now of Romance – continued to escape the historical record, and it's important to remember that this word covers many more languages than simply those of the modern nation states (France, Spain, Italy, Portugal, Romania). A fuller list would include Occitan, the language of southern France, and Sardinian; Galician and Catalan in the northern corners of the Iberian peninsula, as well as the dialects of Venetian, Neapolitan, Sicilian and many others, each of them not versions of modern Italian (as the word 'dialect' in English leads you to believe) but its cousins, independently descended from Latin. Into this list would also go Ladino, the language of the Jewish communities who were expelled from medieval Spain and Portugal and made their way into exile, taking their language with them.

There is a phrase attributed to the linguist Max Weinreich (1894–1969) which goes, 'a language is a dialect with an army and a navy'. The history of Romance is full of powerful forces coalescing and trying to impose their language on others; it is equally full of communities who continue to speak exactly as they wish, ignoring the decrees of those who would like to control them. There is a moment from Irish history which illustrates both sides of this reality, recounted by Raymond Hickey. In 1541 a bill was proclaimed by the Dublin Parliament giving Henry VIII the title King of Ireland, an event attended by representatives from all the major Norman families in Ireland, who had, in the centuries since the Norman conquest, assimilated into the general population and adopted the Irish language. Of all the nobles present, only one of them, the Earl of Ormond, was actually able to understand the English text, and had to translate it for his compatriots. There must have been many similar moments in the Roman empire, made up as it was of many different speech communities. As with Henry VIII here, it's not clear how much the rhetorical bluster of the rulers was backed up by any meaningful or effective attempts to get people to speak one language over another. To the best of our knowledge, Rome's ruling class does not seem to have cared so much what language the general population spoke, as long as its officials and administrators knew Latin.

In the course of more recent European history, certain Romance languages have been officially prioritised at the expense of others. The French state began life in the Middle Ages commanding only the area of Paris and its immediate environs, before extending its control gradually (and militarily) to encompass the borders it has today. This expansion brought the northern French version of Latin, the *langue d'oïl*, to places where Breton was spoken, in the northwest, and to where another version of Latin was spoken, the *langue d'oc*, in the south. The current French Constitution, enacted in 1958, continues to recognise only one official national language, despite the plurality of languages, both Romance and non-Romance, spoken there today. In Italy, at the founding of the modern Italian state in 1860, it is estimated that only around 2.5 per cent of the population spoke Italian – itself a dialect given political prestige and national status – with the majority speaking their own dialects: independent languages, many of which are, in the twenty-first century, spoken by fewer and fewer people. And if you search online, you'll be able to find an advertisement that appeared in a Galician newspaper in the dark days of Franco's dictatorship, in 1942, which barks, in Spanish, *speak correctly*, and goes on to encourage use of Castilian (another name for Spanish):

> Speak correctly. Be patriotic. Do not be coarse. It is the patriotic duty of every true gentleman to speak our official language, Castilian. Long live Spain, Authority and the Language of Cervantes. Spain forever!

The external politics of Latin is well-known: how European imperialism brought French and Spanish and Italian and Portuguese to colonies across the world as instruments of brutality and power. But there is also an internal politics to Latin, within Europe. This is a story of ideas of order being constantly undermined; of centralised authorities (empire, church, and nation state) coming up against an endless diversity of language and lived experience. Some versions of Latin have been sponsored by powerful states, at times in violent and oppressive ways, while others have received little to no official recognition, prestige, or support. Europe has always been home to many different communities, languages, and cultures, not just those idealised Greeks and Romans. The story of Romance is in part the story of human communities continually getting on with things, in and amongst the rulers and powerful classes who dominate the history books, and who try to impose their language onto others. It can help you to critique narrow and unhelpful equations of a kind which are still in vogue, ones like Greece + Rome (Pagan + Christian) = Europe.

*

It would be wrong to view Latin on its journey to modern life simply as a language of international politics, diplomacy, and scholarship, as well as a mainstay of expensive and exclusive schools. The language has always been known to people, encountered on their streets and buildings, in a phrase or motto like *carpe diem* or *quid pro quo*; called upon whenever they have felt the need for words that are in some way elevated, special, or sacred. If you walk from St. Patrick's Cathedral out to Cork Street in Dublin's city centre, you'll pass an old church that has been redeveloped into a shiny new office building. This is St. Luke's, built 1715–16, and once in the heart of the old weaving district between Newmarket and the Coombe, but closed as a church in 1975. On an old stone wall in front of the new office building, an old plaque has survived, recording the lives of two eighteenth-century Dubliners.

Eheu! fugit irreparabile tempus!
Beneath lie the Remains of James
Wallace, who Departed this Life
Feb 13th Anno Domini 1792 & also
those of Deborah his wife, qui obiit
Jan 3 Anno 1792.

As you can see, the inscription has Latin sprinkled through it: *anno Domini* for 'in the year of the Lord', or AD, *qui obiit* for 'who passed away' (as in the word 'obituary'), as well as *anno* for 'in the year'. The first line is more poetic, and features the famous Latin tag *tempus fugit*, or 'time flies', and recalls lines of poetry from the Roman poets Virgil and Horace. 'Alas', it says, 'time flies and doesn't come back'.

James and Deborah may be the parents I've found listed in British Parliamentary records for James Wallace, MP, born 1765, the son of a James Wallace, 'woollen manufacturer, of Meath Street, Dublin', and his wife Deborah Bedford; that would certainly place them in the local parish, and at the right time. If this is the case, then James and Deborah were well-to-do Georgian Dubliners, whose son went to Trinity College and became a barrister and an MP. Similarly to Marcus Caecilius' inscription on the Appian way, however, none of this is mentioned in their memorial, and their common humanity takes precedence over any worldly status. What was once a bustling weaving district is today being reshaped by Dublin's nightmarish accommodation crisis, as new hotels and apartments spring up at the expense of liveable and affordable housing. The inscription has become a strange and counter-cultural witness to the city's past, reminding any Dubliner who stumbles upon it of the different histories of the city and its people, and so perhaps the possibility of different futures. Nor is this kind of memorial limited to Dublin. In 1795, a few years after James and Deborah, a poet named Tadhg

Gaelach Ó Suilleabháin died in Waterford. He was religious man, and wrote religious verse, dying, so the story goes, in the doorway of the city's Catholic cathedral. He had lived in Waterford for many years, and knew Greek and Latin well: he may also be the 'T. Sullivan' who signed himself as a teacher of 'Greek, Latin, book-keeping' at Ballinakill in county Laois in a newspaper advertisement of 1779.

On his death, his friend, fellow poet Donnchadh Rua Mac Conmara (*c.* 1715–1810), composed a Latin poem, in the elegiac metre of the Roman poets, which someone later engraved onto Ó Suilleabháin's headstone in the old graveyard at Ballylaneen, county Waterford. There is a translation into Irish alongside it, but English is nowhere to be seen. Here it is in my translation:

Here lies Tadhg – look this way, traveller,
A little earth covers a famous poet.
Alas, dead he lies, unswerving Fate has won;
His soaring spirit seeks the lofty stars.
Who will sing the praises of the Irish, the deeds of its heroes?
With Gaelach gone, the Irish Muse is silent.
Singing holy songs in learned measures he has passed on;
Victorious now, he has received his sure reward.
By praising God he made beautiful poems,
And now he will sing sweet hymns with gusto.
Weep, ye Muses: your adoptive son is no more,
Eochaigh's descendant is no longer, and all the fields are quiet.
He hoped for peace, so let him rest in peace eternally;
He reaches now the blessed kingdoms of our heavenly Father.

As with those early Roman memorials discussed in Chapter 1, Latin here is still a language in which to commemorate the dead, and Mac Conmara's poem is a moving tribute to his friend. More than that, it speaks to the world of the Penal Laws and the hedge schools we met in Chapter 2, in which Latin's role as a language of high culture became an anti-colonial resource.

In the period between 1800 and the twenty-first century, Latin in Britain and Ireland found and lost an empire, becoming integral to a system of classical education which had always been for the most privileged sections of society, but which now trained civil servants who would go out and run the British empire, particularly in what is now India, Pakistan, Bangladesh, Myanmar, and Sri Lanka. In Ireland, Latin was also the language of the Catholic Church. As with Latin's role in elite education, this was nothing new either, but from the 1920s onwards, that Church in its formal hierarchical structures played an increasingly oppressive role in the new Irish state. All of which is perhaps a way of saying that, like any subject, Latin has been taught well and it has been taught badly; used to prompt students into their own imaginative explorations or to bully them into a callous routine of repetitive rote learning; as an end in itself or as a passport into high society and political influence. This closeness to power was only ceded in the closing decades of the twentieth century, with the decolonisation of the 1950s and 1960s, and the democratic moment of the 1960s in particular opening up formal, state-sponsored education to a broader section of society. Latin is still taught in expensive schools, but it no longer has the political capital that it once did, and this is no bad thing. Meaningful and creative arts education should be available to every citizen, if they want it: this doesn't have to be Latin, and, if it is, it should be offered and not imposed.

Having said that, it would be remiss of me not to end with what Latin does well, particularly in the hands of a good teacher, of which there are many. Looking at the prospects of the Italian education system in the 1930s – then, as now, heavily based in Greek and Latin – Antonio Gramsci recognised that if Greek and Latin went, then something would be lost that would have to be provided in some other form:

> Pupils did not learn Latin and Greek in order to be able to speak them, to become waiters, interpreters or commercial letter-writers. They learnt them in order to know at first hand the civilisation of Greece and Rome – a civilisation that was a necessary precondition of our modern civilisation: in other words: they learnt them in order to be themselves and to know themselves consciously.

I don't include this quotation to celebrate Greek and Latin at the expense of professional or artisanal careers, and I hesitate to include it at all because the word 'civilisation' has been so often used to promote the worst kind of imperial politics. But that is not, I think, what Gramsci means. He means that what the study of the past (and it doesn't – I would add – have to be the Latin past) can give you is an historical understanding, a 'plunge into history'; it can help you co-ordinate yourself in the world, and perhaps lead to some measure of self-understanding. Formal education, and this kind of formal education in particular, is often a luxury few can afford, but the reasons for this are political, not inevitable. The Roman empire has shaped European history, good and bad, and people in my experience are continually fascinated by it, whether inside or outside the classroom.

In an Irish context, the poet Eavan Boland wrote about her own experience of learning Latin, and the way it gave her access to the kind of imaginative and creative resources I've been talking about. She learnt it at Holy Child school in Killiney, county Dublin, as a teenager, with a woman whom she initially found as intimidating and difficult as the language itself. The key moment came when she realised her teacher's passion for her subject and began to apply herself, the relationship between teacher and student – and between student and subject – suddenly transformed. She described the moment when things clicked:

> Some time in my last year – although this is a figurative use of time – I began to understand something. It was something about the economy of it all: the way the ablative absolute gathered and compressed time. One day – again figuratively – it was a burdensome piece of grammar. The next, with hardly any warning, it was a messenger with quick heels and a bright face. I began to understand the system of a language which could make such a construct: that – although I had no such words for it – it stood against the disorders of love or history, that it had been made to describe bridges and define governments. At that point of my adulthood, where the words I wrote on a page were nothing but inexact, the precision and force of this construct were both moving and healing.

For Boland, her experience with Latin was a decisive one in making her a poet, showing her at close quarters what language could do. She goes on to quote her poem 'The Latin Lesson', in which classmates crush words together for their fragrance, discovering the power of translation. Figures of authority loom as the narrator, a young woman, discovers for herself worlds of new experience; the process is both mundane and magical. 'We translate all the time, everywhere we are', Boland concludes. This kind of transformative experience in school, often linked to the memory of an inspirational teacher, is something many people can relate to, in different subjects.

Latin continues to exist outside schools and universities, too, a useful curiosity and, sometimes, a way of saying something special and important. Dublin is full of bits of Latin, sometimes big and proud like the lettering above a church, sometimes small and hidden away, like the memorial to the Wallaces. Less obvious to the untrained eye is how many modern companies and brands take their names from Latin words; whoever made these names has gone to Latin for its authority and prestige, and usually to words that imply size and strength. Latin is still used by doctors, lawyers, and gardeners across the world, in the gardeners' case to identify precise varieties of plants and trees, in the binomial system created by the Swedish botanist Carl Linnaeus (1707–78). This system of classification gives each tree, plant, or shrub its own two-part Latin name, one for the *genus* and one for the *species*. Lavender, for instance, is *Lavandula*, and one of its varieties *Lavandula angustifolia* ('narrow-leaf'): one theory has it that *Lavandula* got its name from the Latin verb *lavare*, to wash, owing to its use in perfuming and infusions through the centuries. Your star-sign is in Latin, whether or not you read your horoscope. These words are part of an ancient tradition of interpreting the movement of the sun through the sky, stretching back through ancient Rome and Greece to Babylon. They might be the most well-known Latin words of all.

aries, 'ram'
taurus, 'bull'
gemini, 'twins'
cancer, 'crab'
leo, 'lion'
virgo, 'virgin'
libra, 'scales'
scorpio, 'scorpion'
sagittarius, 'archer' (*sagitta*, 'arrow')
capricornus, 'capricorn' (*caper*, 'goat', *cornu*, 'horn')
aquarius, 'water-bearer' (*aqua*, 'water')
pisces, 'fish'

For some people, Latin is still the go-to language for a new tattoo, or the grave of a loved one. It's part of the furniture of modern life.

*

Over the course of 2020 I began listening to music from Latin America: dance and pop tunes, mainly, love songs from Mexico and Chile and Cuba. I loved the freedom and vitality of the music, the way it made me want to get up and dance around the room. Latin America is a useful case study when thinking about Latin and Romance in modern times: a place where the worst kinds of power have had terrible influence, yet also a place where ideas of democratic solidarity have flourished in response. The name 'Latin America' is thought to have originated as the arrogant generalisation of European diplomats in the nineteenth century, eager to stake their claim to the continent and its resources, yet even as this was being done, in the 1850s and 1860s, others were already using the term to put forward an anti-imperial politics of their own. Today, Spanish and Portuguese are spoken by millions of people in Latin America, but so too are many different indigenous languages – like Quechua, Aymara, and Nahuatl – whose communities have survived the apocalypses of previous centuries. In the Yucatán peninsula in eastern Mexico, the indigenous Maya language has influenced the Spanish spoken in the region, and Spanish has influenced in turn its indigenous counterpart. People moving northward in search of safety, or simply a better life, bring this linguistic diversity with them as they go. They also carry the songs, in the words of Irish poet Moya Cannon, proving that what is true for language is true also for music, the Latin American traditions themselves a fusion of European, African, and indigenous forms. When I listen to *boleros*, watch a film like *The Golden Dream*, or see women protesting for their lives with the words of Susana Chávez Castillo (1974–2011) – *ni una mujer menos, ni una muerta más* ('not one woman less, not one more woman dead') – I can see the poetry and the politics and the complexity of Latin, past and present, side by side.

There is always the risk of generalising unhelpfully about a large and very diverse part of the world. But thinking about Latin America, and in particular listening to its music, made me realise that this language (I was listening to songs in Spanish) was just as much 'Latin' as the language of verbs and nouns and ancient Romans that I had first learnt in school. This is, on one level, completely obvious: everyone knows that the Romance languages come from Latin. But the point is that I was learning it for myself (true education is self-education, Mary Wollstonecraft says), and learning what I've tried to show you in this essay: that Latin and Romance are not different things, but rather different versions of the same thing. I was able to take some of the lyrics of these songs and – in a very amateur way – reverse engineer them back into Latin, helped by the fact that the links between Spanish and Latin are more obvious to the untrained eye than they are in other Romance languages. I realised, most importantly of all, that this language that I teach and study has nothing – necessarily – to do with empires and generals and powerful institutions; nothing, even, to do with education. They are contained within it, not it within them. Latin is still a language of ordinary people, from Bucharest to the Bronx and from Sicily to São Paulo, a language that you can hear in each of its five major versions on the streets of Dublin. If you were to ask me what 'living' Latin means, I might point you to a conversation at a junction or a bus-stop in one of these languages. History is about making connections.

Notes, with Further Reading, Listening and Watching

Preface

Adams, J. N., 'Diversity and the Latin language', blog post for *Càtedra UNESCO de Diversitat Lingüistica i Cultural, Institut d'Estudis Catalans*, Barcelona, 15 July 2020: https://catedra-unesco.espais.iec.cat/en/2020/07/15/47-diversity-and-the-latin-language/, last accessed 24.5.23.

Rich, Adrienne, *Arts of the Possible: Essays and Conversations* (New York: Norton and co., 2001) p. 167.

Zinn, Howard, *A People's History of the United States* (New York: Harper Collins, 2015).

Chapter 1: The Latin of Ordinary People

Alexievich, Svetlana, 'busy doing inhumanly human things': *The Unwomanly Face of War*, translated by Richard Pevear and Larissa Volokhonsky (London: Penguin, 2017), p. xvi.

The Latin of ordinary people

Adams, J. N., *An Anthology of Informal Latin, 200 BC – AD 900: Fifty Texts with Translations and Linguistic Commentary* (Cambridge, 2016), plus, for those interested, three specialist works: *Bilingualism and the Latin Language* (Cambridge, 2003), *The Regional Diversification of Latin, 200 BC – AD 600* (Cambridge, 2007) and *Social Variation and the Latin Language* (Cambridge, 2013).

Arnove, Anthony (ed.), *The Essential Chomsky* (London: The Bodley Head, 2008).

Berwick, R. C, and Chomsky, N., *Why Only Us: Language and Evolution* (Cambridge, MA: MIT Press, 2016).

Roy, Arundhati, 'The End of Imagination', in *My Seditious Heart: Collected Non-Fiction* (London: Hamish Hamilton, 2019) pp. 1–23, at p. 9.

Stevens, Wallace, 'The Man with the Blue Guitar', in *The Collected Poems of Wallace Stevens* (London: Faber, 1955), pp. 165–84.

'veni, vidi, vici'

Holiday, Billie, 'These Foolish Things (Remind Me of You)', recorded 30 June 1936, on *Lady Day: The Complete Billie Holiday on Columbia 1933–1944* (Columbia/Legacy, 2001).

Mac Domhnaill, Seán Clárach, 'Bímse buan ar buairt gach ló'/ 'My Heart is Sore with Sorrow Deep', text edited by Risteárd Ó Foghludha with translation by Colm Breathnach, in Angela Bourke and others (eds.), *The Field Day Anthology of Irish Writing. Volume IV: Irish Women's Writing and Traditions* (Cork: Cork University Press/Field Day, 2002), pp. 285–6.

Suetonius, *Lives of the Caesars, Volume I: Julius. Augustus. Tiberius. Gaius. Caligula,* translated by J. C. Rolfe, revised edition (Cambridge: MA: Harvard University Press, 1998), p. 81.

Zinn, Howard and Suarez, Ray, *Truth Has a Power of Its Own: Conversations about A People's History* (New York: The New Press, 2019), pp. 16–18.

Irish English

Hickey, Raymond, *Irish English: History and present-day forms* (Cambridge, 2007), and *Sociolinguistics in Ireland* (London: Palgrave Macmillan, 2016).

The Palestrina brooch

Wallace, Rex, 'The Latin Alphabet and Orthography', pp. 7–28, and John Penney, 'Archaic and Old Latin', pp. 220–35, both in J. Clackson (ed.), *A Companion to the Latin Language* (Chichester: Wiley-Blackwell, 2011).

The artisans (at Ravenna, Rome, Ostia and Pompeii)

Clarke, John R., *Art in the Lives of Ordinary Romans: Visual Representation and Non-Elite Viewers in Italy, 100 B.C. – A.D. 315* (Berkeley, CA:

University of California Press, 2003), for all texts and translations featured.

Delamarre, Xavier, 'Longidienus, *faber navalis* à Ravenne, le toponyme Lombard et le thème longo- *navire* en vieux celtique', in *Zeitschrift für celtische Philologie*, vol. 60 no. 1 (2013) pp.19–26.

Livy, Book 6, Chapter 25, in *History of Rome, Volume III: Books 5-7*, translated by B. O. Foster (Cambridge, MA: Harvard University Press, 1924) p. 285, with many other translations available in print and online.

The Pietrabbondante roof tile

Adams, J. N., *Social Variation and the Latin Language* (Cambridge, 2013), pp. 124–7, drawing on Paolo Poccetti, *Nuovi documenti italici* (Pisa, 1979), p. 21.

Cooley, Alison E. (ed.), *Res Gestae Divi Augusti: Text, Translation and Commentary* (Cambridge, 2009), section 25.2, pp. 89, 216–17, for Octavian's 'all Italy' claim.

Gabba, Emilio, 'Rome and Italy: The Social War', in J. A. Crook, A. Lintott, and E. Rawson (eds), *The Cambridge Ancient History, Volume IX: The Last Age of the Roman Republic, 146–43 B.C.* (Cambridge, 1994), second edition, pp. 104–28.

McDonald, Katherine, 'Four footprints, two languages, one tile', blog post, 14 January 2016: https://katherinemcdonald.net/2016/01/14/four-footprints-two-languages-one-tile/, last accessed 24.5.23.

The Roman epitaphs

Courtney, Edward, *Musa Lapidaria. A Selection of Latin Verse Inscriptions* (Atlanta, GA: Scholars Press, 1995), for translations of all the Roman epitaphs except Marcus Caecilius.

Warmington, E. H. (ed.), *Remains of Old Latin, Volume IV: Archaic Inscriptions* (Cambridge, MA: Harvard University Press, 1940), p. 11, for translation of the Marcus Caecilius inscription.

Pompeii and Herculaneum

Adams, J. N., 'genuinely popular Latin': *An Anthology of Informal Latin*, p. 226.

Clackson, James, 'The language of a Pompeian tavern: submerged Latin?' in J. N. Adams and Nigel Vincent (eds), *Early and late Latin: continuity or change?* (Cambridge, 2016), pp. 69–86.

Clarke, John R., *Art in the Lives of Ordinary Romans*, for the procession, the clothmakers, and the couple from the bakery complex.

Cooley, Alison E., and Cooley, M. G. L., *Pompeii and Herculaneum: A Sourcebook*, second edition (London: Routledge, 2014), for all graffiti translations featured, except the apology to the host, for which see Milnor, below, and the translation of wall quip ('I'm amazed . . .'), which is mine.

Graverini, Luca, 'Ovidian Graffiti: Love, Genre and Gender on a Wall in Pompeii. A New Study of *CIL IV. 5296/CLE 950*', in *Incontri di filologia classica*, vol. 12 (2012–2013) pp. 1–28.

Milnor, Kristina, *Graffiti and the Literary Landscape in Roman Pompeii* (Oxford, 2014).

Norton, Rictor, *Myth of the Modern Homosexual: Queer History and the Search for Cultural Unity* (London: Bloomsbury, 2016).

Vindolanda

Bowman, Alan K., *Life and Letters on the Roman Frontier: Vindolanda and its People* (London: British Museum Press, 2003).

Rich, Adrienne, 'The Burning of Paper Instead of Children', in *Collected Early Poems, 1950–1970* (New York: Norton and co., 1993), pp. 363–6.

Roman Inscriptions of Britain, online database, managed by The University of Nottingham and The University of Oxford, 2014–, https://romaninscriptionsofbritain.org/, last accessed 24.5.23. You can find text, translation, and commentary for the sources mentioned by searching the following numbers in the search-box:

(i) the weather: *Tab. Vindol.* 234

(ii) reference to the indigenous population: *Tab. Vindol.* 164

(iii) a letter of recommendation: *Tab. Vindol.* 250

(iv) lines from Virgil: *Tab. Vindol.* 452, 854

(v) request for beer: *Tab. Vindol.* 628

(vi) *caballus* over *equus* for 'horse': *Tab. Vindol.* 890

(vii) Claudia Severa's letter: *Tab. Vindol.* 291

Bath

Roman Inscriptions of Britain, online database. For text, translation and commentary, search the following:

(i) The Palmyrene memorial: *RIB* 1065

(ii) The 'Vilbia' curse tablet: *RIB* 154

Tomlin, Roger, 'The Curse Tablets', in B. Cunliffe (ed.), *The Temple of Sulis Minerva at Bath. Volume 2: The Finds from the Sacred Spring* (Oxford: OUCA, 1988) pp. 59–278; see p. 123 for the tablet about the theft of the cloak.

Egeria's travels

Adams, J. N., *The Regional Diversification of Latin 200 BC – AD 600* (Cambridge, 2007), pp. 342–53.

Erhart, Victoria, *Itinerarium Egeriae: A Pilgrim's Journey*, in Churchill, L. J., Brown, P. R. and Jeffrey, Jane E., *Women Writing Latin: From Roman Antiquity to Modern Europe* (London: Routledge, 2002), 3 vols, volume 1, pp. 165–82.

Wilkinson, John, *Egeria's Travels*, 3rd edition (Warminster: Aris and Phillips, 1999), for the translations featured here.

Jerome and the Vulgate Bible

The Holy Bible. New International Version (London: Hodder and Stoughton, 1980): translations taken from this edition.

Bogaert, Pierre-Maurice, 'The Latin Bible', in J. C. Paget and J. Schaper (eds), *The New Cambridge History of the Bible: From The Beginnings to 600* (Cambridge, 2013), pp. 505–26.

Dürer, Albrecht, *Saint Jerome in His Study*, engraving, 1514, in the collection of The Metropolitan Museum of Art, New York, https://www.metmuseum.org/art/collection/search/336229, last accessed 26 May 2023.

Harvey Jr., Paul B., 'Vulgate and Other Ancient Latin Translations', in M. D. Coogan (ed.), *The Oxford Encyclopedia of the Books of the Bible*, online edition (Oxford, 2011).

Ní Chuilleanáin, Eiléan, 'To Niall Woods and Xenya Ostrovskaya, Married in Dublin on 9 September 2009', in *The Sun-fish* (Oldcastle, co. Meath: Gallery Press, 2009), available at the website of the Griffin Poetry Prize, https://griffinpoetryprize.com/poem/to-niall-woods-and-xenya-ostrovskaia-married-in-dublin-on-9-september-2009/, last accessed 26 May 2023.

The conclusion

Graeber, David, *Fragments of An Anarchist Anthropology* (Chicago: Prickly Paradigm Press, 2004), p. 47.

Heaney, Seamus, *Human Chain* (London: Faber, 2010).

Chapter 2: Pop Classics

Smyth, J., 'cotton, silk, woollen and linen weavers . . .': *The Men of No Property: Irish Radicals and Popular Politics in the Late Eighteenth Century* (Dublin: Gill and Macmillan, 1992) p. 124.

Catullus, Petronius and Sulpicia

Bowe, Nicola, *Harry Clarke: The Life and Work, revised edition* (Dublin: History Press, 2012).

Catullus, *The Complete Poems*, translated by Guy Lee (Oxford, 2008), and for an expert account of the Catullan manuscript tradition, J. L. Butrica, 'History and Transmission of the Text', in M. B. Skinner (ed.), *A Companion to Catullus* (Oxford: Blackwell, 2007), pp. 13–34.

Keith, Alison, 'Critical Trends in Interpreting Sulpicia', *The Classical World* vol. 100 no. 1, Fall 2006, pp. 3–10.

Lyne, Oliver, '[Tibullus] Book 3 and Sulpicia 1', in *Collected Papers on Latin Literature*, edited by Stephen Harrison (Oxford, 2007).

Petronius, *Satyricon*, edited and translated by Gareth Schmeling (Cambridge, MA: Harvard University Press, 2020), pp. 215–17. Translation from this edition, slightly edited.

Satyricon (dir. Federico Fellini, Italy, 1969).

Scott Fitzgerald, F., *The Great Gatsby* (London: Penguin Classics, 2018).

Plautus, Terence and their reception

'one ancient critic': Aelius Stilo, who is supposed to have said that 'the Muses would have talked like Plautus if they had chosen to speak Latin'. See Quintilian, *The Orator's Education* (Cambridge, MA: Harvard University Press, 2001), 10 January 1999, translated by Donald A. Russell.

Angelou, Maya, 'I am human', 5 March 2013, https://www.youtube.com/watch?v=ePodNjrVSsk&t, last accessed 24 May 2023.

Baldwin, James, *The Fire Next Time* (London: Penguin, 1964), p. 42.

Barnard, John Levi, *Empire of Ruin: Black Classicism and American Imperial Culture* (New York: Oxford University Press, 2018).

Beatley, Meaghan, 'The shocking rape trial that galvanised Spain's feminists – and the far right', *The Guardian*, 23 April 2019, https://www.theguardian.com/world/2019/apr/23/wolf-pack-case-spain-feminism-far-right-vox, last accessed 26 May 2023.

Bliss, Panti, Anderssen, Erin and O'Toole, Emer, 'Gender Performed – A conversation about sex, gender, theatre, and politics', Concordia University, Montreal, 19 February 2016, https://www.youtube.com/watch?v=19P-6noFIJI, last accessed 24 May 2023.

Cook, William W. and Tatum, James, *African American Writers of the Classical Tradition* (Chicago, 2010).

Cat on a Hot Tin Roof (dir. Richard Brooks, United States, 1958), based on Tennessee Williams' 1955 play of the same name.

Hedda Gabler (dir. Paul Hoffman, United States, 1963), based on Henrik Ibsen's 1891 play of the same name.

Hughes, Langston, 'Prelude to Our Age: A Negro History Poem', in Arnold Rampersand (ed.), *The Collected Works of Langston Hughes, Volume 3. The Poems: 1951–1967* (Columbia, MO: University of Missouri Press, 2001), pp. 191–7.

McCarthy, Kathleen, *Slaves, Masters, and the Art of Authority in Plautine Comedy* (Princeton, NJ, 2000).

Murtagh, Peter, 'The full story of the midlands rape trial', *The Irish Times*, 2 June 2022.

Parallel Mothers (dir. P. Almodóvar, Spain, 2021).

Plautus, edited and translated by Wolfgang de Melo, 5 vols (Cambridge, MA: Harvard University Press, 2011–13).

Richlin, Amy, *Slave Theater in the Roman Republic: Slave Theatre and Popular Comedy* (Cambridge, 2019).

Southern, Eileen, *The Music of Black Americans*, 3rd edition (NY: Norton and Co., 1997).

Terence, edited and translated by John Barsby, 2 vols (Cambridge, MA: Harvard University Press, 2001).

West, Cornel, 'Religion and the Left' and 'On Afro-American Music: From Bebop to Rap', in *The Cornel West Reader* (New York: *Civitas*, 1999).

Wheatley, Phillis, 'To Maecenas', in *Poems on Various Subject, Religious and Moral and A Memoir of Phillis Wheatley, A Native African and A Slave* (London: Renard Press, 2020), pp. 13–14, with Terence footnote on p. 14.

Wilde, Oscar, *The Importance of Being Earnest: A Trivial Comedy for Serious People*, in Isobel Murray (ed.), *Oscar Wilde: The Major Works*, new edition (Oxford, 2000), p. 512.

Virgil and his reception

'Winnie the Pooh and Christopher Robin': from a lecture on Virgil and Dante I attended given by Cormac Ó Cuilleanáin, Professor Emeritus of Italian at TCD.

Ali, Tariq, 'Winged Words', in *The London Review of Books* vol. 43 no. 12, 17 June 2021, https://www.lrb.co.uk/the-paper/v43/n12/tariq-ali/winged-words, last accessed 26 May 2023.

Burrow, Colin, 'Shakespeare and humanistic culture', in C. Martindale and A. B. Taylor (eds), *Shakespeare and the Classics* (Cambridge, 2004), pp. 9–32.

Cáceres, Berta, acceptance speech for the 2015 Goldman Environmental Prize, https://www.youtube.com/watch?v=AR1kwx8b0ms, with further information at: https://www.goldmanprize.org/recipient/berta-caceres/, links last accessed 24 May 2023.

Cervantes, Miguel De, *Don Quixote*, translated by John Rutherford (London: Penguin, 2003).

Comparetti, Domenico, *Virgilio nel medio evo*, 2 vols (Livorno, 1872), English edition translated by E. Benecke as *Vergil in the Middle Ages* (London, 1895) and reissued in 1997 by Princeton University Press, with an introduction by J. M. Ziolkowski.

Ferrante, Elena, *The Story of the Lost Child*, translated by Ann Goldstein (New York: Europa Editions, 2015), pp. 466–7.

Friel, Brian, *Translations* (London: Faber, 1981).

Furlong, Nicholas, 'Murphy, John', *Dictionary of Irish Biography*, online edition, Royal Irish Academy, Dublin, https://www.dib.ie/biography/murphy-john-a6081, last accessed 24 May 2023.

Gigante, Marcello, 'Vergil in the Shadow of Vesuvius', in D. Armstrong, J. Fish, P. A. Johnston, and M. B. Skinner (eds), *Vergil, Philodemus, and the Augustans* (Austin, TX: University of Texas Press, 2004), pp. 85–99.

Hall, Edith and Stead, Henry, *A People's History of Classics: Class and Greco-Roman Antiquity in Britain and Ireland 1689–1939* (Routledge: Abingdon, 2020), Chapter 10.

Heaney, Seamus, *Aeneid VI* (London: Faber, 2016), p. 51.

Kelly, Samantha, *The Cronaca di Partenope: An Introduction to and Critical Edition of the First Vernacular History of Naples (c. 1350)* (Leiden: Brill, 2011).

Klein, Naomi and Schwarz, Jon, '*Don't Look Up* and Fighting Capitalism with Naomi Klein', podcast with transcription, *The Intercept*, 12 January 2022, https://theintercept.com/2022/01/12/intercepted-podcast-dont-look-up-naomi-klein/, last accessed 24 May 2023.

Mahon, Derek, 'The Rain Forest' and 'Trump Time', from *Against the Clock* (Oldcastle, co. Meath: Gallery Press, 2018).

Mandelbaum, Allen, *Dante: Purgatorio* (Berkeley, CA, 2008), XXX. 43–54, available via the *Digital Dante* project (Columbia University, New York), https://digitaldante.columbia.edu/, last accessed 24 May 2023.

McElduff, Siobhán, 'Irish Didos: Empire, Gender, and Class in the Irish Popular Tradition to Frank McGuinness's *Carthaginians*', in Isabelle Torrance and Donncha O'Rourke (eds), *Classics and Irish Politics, 1916–2016* (Oxford, 2020), pp. 268–90.

McManus, Antonia, *The Irish Hedge School and Its Books, 1695–1831* (Dublin: Four Courts Press, 2004).

Moryson, Fynes, *An history of Ireland, from the year 1599, to 1603. With a short narration of the state of the kingdom from the year 1169. To which is added, A description of Ireland* (Dublin: S. Powell, 1735), 2 vols, vol. 1 p. 115.

Nelson, E. C. and Walsh, W. F., *Trees of Ireland: Native and Naturalized* (Dublin: Lilliput Press, 1993), pp. 139–40.

O'Higgins, Laurie, *The Irish Classical Self: Poets and Poor Scholars in the Eighteenth and Nineteenth Centuries* (Oxford, 2017), p. 6.

Shakespeare, William, *Hamlet*, edited by T. J. B. Spencer, Penguin Classics reissue (London: Penguin, 2005), p. 59.

Virgil, *Aeneid*, translated by H. R. Fairclough and revised by G. P. Goold, 2 vols (Cambridge, MA: Harvard University Press), with many other translations available in print and online.

Ovid; Orpheus and Eurydice

Addison, Joseph, *The Spectator*, no. 417, Saturday June 28, 1712, in D. F. Bond (ed.) *Critical Essays from the Spectator by Joseph Addison* (Oxford, 1970).

Arcade Fire, 'Awful Sound (Oh Eurydice)' and 'It's Never Over (Hey Orpheus)' on *Reflektor* (Sonovox/Merge, 2013).

Atwood, Margaret, 'Orpheus (1)', 'Eurydice', and 'Orpheus (2)', in *Poems 1976–1986* (London: Virago Press, 1992).

Berger, John, 'Forthflowing on a Joycean Tide', in *Landscapes: John Berger on Art* edited by Tom Overton (London: Verso: 2018), p. 86.

Boland, Eavan, 'The Pomegranate', in *New Collected Poems* (Manchester: Carcanet, 2005), pp. 215–16, and 'Eurydice Speaks', in *A Woman Without Country* (Manchester: Carcanet, 2014) p. 21.

Galán, Lía, 'El mito de Orfeo en el teatro argentino contemporáneo: La casa sin sosiego de Griselda Gambaro', in A. Rubén Pricco and S. Maris Moro (eds), *Pervivencia del mundo clásico en la literatura: tradición y relecturas* (Coimbra: Coimbra University Press, 2017), pp. 249–60.

La casa sin sosiego/The House Without Calm, words by Griselda Gambaro (b. 1928) and music by Gerardo Gandini (1936–2013).

Le Guin, Ursula K., *Dreams Must Explain Themselves: The Selected Non-Fiction of Ursula K. Le Guin* (London: Gollancz, 2018), pp. 4 and 46.

Hadestown, music, lyrics, and book by Anaïs Mitchell, dir. Rachel Chavkin, Off-Broadway 2016/Broadway 2019.

Heaney, Seamus, 'The Underground', in *Station Island* (London: Faber, 1984), p. 13.

Hozier, 'Talk', on *Wasteland, Baby!* (Rubyworks/Island, 2019).

Marx, Karl, *Capital: Volume 1* (London: Penguin, 2011).

Miłosz, Czesław, 'Orpheus and Eurydice', in *Selected and Last Poems 1931–2004* (London: Penguin, 2006), pp. 260–3.

Monteverdi, Claudio, *L'Orfeo* (SV 318, first performed Mantua, Italy, 1607).

Orfeu Negro/Black Orpheus (dir. Marcel Camus, France, 1959).

Orphée/Orpheus (dir. Jean Cocteau, France, 1950).

Ovid, *Metamorphoses*, translated by A. S. Kline (University of Virginia, 2000), https://ovid.lib.virginia.edu/trans/Ovhome.htm, last accessed 26 May 2023, with many more translations available in print and online.

Portrait of a Lady on Fire/Portrait de la jeune fille en feu (dir. Céline Sciamma, France, 2019), with the relevant clip at: https://www.youtube.com/watch?v=PVINp97hgvc, last accessed 24 May 2023.

Roy, Arundhati, 'The Graveyard Talks Back: Fiction in the Time of Fake News', in *Azadi: Freedom, Fascism, Fiction* (London: Penguin, 2020), pp. 150–95.

Sirr, Peter, 'Don't Look Back: Poetry and Retrieval', *The Cat Flap* blog, 2 December 2015, http://petersirr.blogspot.com/2015/12/dont-look-back-poetry-and-retrieval.html, last accessed 24 May 2023.

Virgil, *Georgics*, translated by H. R. Fairclough and revised by G. P. Goold (Cambridge, MA: Harvard University Press), with many other translations available in print and online.

Chapter 3 Latin to Romance

Learning Latin

Berger, John, 'On the Economy of the Dead', *Harpers*, September 2008 issue, https://harpers.org/archive/2008/09/on-the-economy-of-the-dead/, last accessed 24 May 2023.

G. K. Chesterton, *Orthodoxy* (London: John Lane, 1908), p. 85.

Dickey, Eleanor, *Learning Latin the ancient way: Latin textbooks from the ancient world* (Cambridge, 2016).

Virgil, *Aeneid*, book 2.

Roger Wright's work

A Sociophilological Study of Late Latin (Utrecht: Brepols, 2002), with shorter treatments in Adam Ledgeway and Martin Maiden (eds), *The Oxford Guide to the Romance Languages* (Oxford, 2016), pp. 14–23, and Martin Maiden, John Charles Smith, and Adam Ledgeway (eds) *The Cambridge History of the Romance Languages* (Cambridge, 2013, 2 vols), vol. 2, pp. 107–24.

Augustine, Gerald of Wales, 'Phoebus was gone . . .'

Augustine, *Confessions*, 2 vols, translated by Carolyn J.-B. Hammond (Cambridge, MA: Harvard University Press, 2014 and 2016), with many other translations available.

Boland, Eavan, 'Phoebus was gone, all gone, his journey over', translation with translator's note, in *Poetry*, April 2008 issue, Chicago, IL, available at https://www.poetryfoundation.org/poetrymagazine/poems/50915/phoebus-was-gone-all-gone-his-journey-over, last accessed 24 May 2023.

Dimock, James F. (ed.), *Giraldi Cambrensis Opera* ['The Works of Gerald of Wales'], vol. 5 (London: Longmans, Green and co., 1867), *Topographia Hibernica* ['Topography of Ireland'], preface, 1.4, and 3.10 (translations my own).

Dronke, Peter, 'Learned Lyric and Popular Ballad in the Early Middle Ages', in *The Medieval Poet and His World* (Rome: Edizioni di Storia e Letteratura, 1984), pp. 167–208.

Ní Mhaonaigh, Máire, 'Perception and Reality: Ireland *c.* 980–1229', in Brendan Smith (ed.), *The Cambridge History of Ireland. Volume 1: 600–1500* (Cambridge, 2018), pp. 131–56, at pp. 143–4 (for Gerald of Wales' assertion that the Irish 'live like beasts').

O'Donnell, James J., *Augustine: Confessions*, 3 vols (Oxford: Clarendon Press, 1992), volume 2, p. 8.

Stevenson, Jane, *Women Latin poets: language, gender, and authority, from antiquity to the eighteenth century* (Oxford, 2008), p. 116.

Old Latin Gospels, the Spanish slate, the Roman catacomb graffito

Adams, J. N., *An Anthology of Informal Latin*, pp. 564–71, based on Isabel Velázquez Soriano, *Las pizarras visigodas (Entre el latín y su disgregación: la lengua hablada en Hispania, siglos VI–VIII)* (Burgos, Real Academia Española, 2004).

Burton, Philip, *The Old Latin Gospels: a study of their texts and language* (Oxford: Oxford University Press, 2000), pp. 157–71.

Petrucci, Livio, 'Il problema delle origini e i più antichi testi italiani', in Luca Serianni and Pietro Trifone (eds), *Storia della lingua italiana* (Turin, 1994), vol. 3, pp. 5–73, at pp. 25–6.

Elizabeth I, Galileo, Spinoza

Berger, John, *Bento's Sketchbook* (London: Verso, 2015).

Butterfield, David, 'Neo-Latin', in J. Clackson (ed.), *A Companion to the Latin Language* (Chichester: Wiley-Blackwell, 2011), pp. 303–18.

Drake, Stillman, *Galileo: A Very Short Introduction* (Oxford, 2001), preface, for the quote about philosophy.

Flood, Alison, 'Messy handwriting reveals mystery translator: Queen Elizabeth I', *The Guardian*, 29 November 2019, https://www.theguardian.com/books/2019/nov/29/handwriting-identifies-elizabeth-i-tacitus-translation, last accessed 26 May 2023.

Galilei, Galileo, *Dialogue Concerning the Two Chief World Systems – Ptolemaic & Copernican*, translated by Stillman Drake, 2nd edition (Berkeley, CA, 1967).

Klever, Wim, 'Spinoza's life and works', in Don Garrett (ed.), *The Cambridge Companion to Spinoza* (Cambridge, 1996), pp. 13–60.

Ó Macháin, Pádraig (ed.), 'Irish Primer', *Irish Script on Screen*, online resource, Dublin Institute of Advanced Studies, at https://www.isos.dias.ie/MARSH/Irish_Primer.html, last accessed 24 May 2023.

Spinoza, *Ethics, and Treatise on the Correction of the Intellect*, translated by Andrew Boyle, revised by George H. R. Parkinson (London: Orion, 1993).

Spinoza, *Theological-Political Treatise*, edited by Jonathan Israel, translated by Michael Silverthorne and Jonathan Israel (Cambridge, 2007).

Latin to Romance

Beswick, Jaine E., *Regional Nationalism in Spain: Language Use and Ethnic Identity in Galicia* (Clevedon: Multilingual Matters Ltd, 2007) p. 79 for text and translation of the Galician newspaper ad, quoting X. R. Freixeiro Mato, *Lingua Galega: Normalidade e Conflito* (Santiago de Compostela: Edicións Laiovento, 1997), p. 90.

Dante, *De vulgari eloquentia*, edited and translated by Steve Botterill (Cambridge: University of Cambridge Press, 1996).

Elcock, W. D., *The Romance Languages*, new and revised edition (London: Faber, 1975).

Raymond Hickey, *Irish English*, p. 34.

Repetti, Lori, 'Teaching about the Other Italian Languages: Dialectology in the Italian Curriculum', *Italica* vol. 73 no. 4 (1996), pp. 508–15.

Memorials, education and Latin into the twenty-first century

Two pieces of Latin suggested by the memorial to the Wallaces:

Sed fugit interea, fugit inreparabile tempus . . .
'But meanwhile time is flying, time that will not come again . . .'
(Virgil, *Georgics*, 3.284, my translation)

Eheu fugaces, Postume, Postume,
labuntur anni . . .
'Oh Postumus, the fleeing years are slipping by . . .'
(Horace, *Odes* 2.14.1–2, my translation)

Boland, Eavan, 'The Living Language', *Classics Ireland* vol. 25 (2018), pp. 81–97.

Fisher, R. R. (ed.), 'Wallace, Thomas II (1765–1847), of Belfield, Donnybrook, co. Dublin', in *The History of Parliament: The House of Commons 1820–1832* (Cambridge: Cambridge University Press), online edition, https://www.historyofparliamentonline.org/volume/1820-1832/member/wallace-thomas-ii-1765-1847, last accessed 24 May 2023.

Gramsci, Antonio, quoted in Q. Hoare and G. Nowell-Smith (eds), *Selections from the Prison Notebooks of Antonio Gramsci* (New York: International Publishers, 1971), pp. 182–5.

Hyde, Douglas, *A Literary History of Ireland: From Earliest Times to the Present Day*, new edition, edited by Brian Ó Cuív (London: Ernest Benn,

1967), p. 603, where he explains the epithet *Eochades* as 'the descendant of Eochaigh Muighmheadhoin, father of Niall of the Nine Hostages'.

Morley, Vincent, 'Mac Conmara, Donnchadh "Rua"', *Dictionary of Irish Biography*, online edition, Royal Irish Academy, Dublin: https://www.dib.ie/biography/mac-conmara-donnchadh-rua-a5021, last accessed 24 May 2023.

Morley, Vincent, 'Ó Suilleabháin, Tadhg "Gaelach"', *Dictionary of Irish Biography*, Royal Irish Academy, online edition, Dublin: https://www.dib.ie/biography/o-suilleabhain-tadhg-gaelach-a6444, last accessed 24 May 2023.

Vasunia, Phiroze, *The Classics and Colonial India* (Oxford, 2013).

Latin America

Cannon, Moya, 'Carrying the Songs', from *Carrying the Songs* (Manchester: Carcanet, 2007), available online at https://moyacannon.ie/books/carrying-the-songs/, last accessed 29 May 2023.

Galeano, Eduardo, *Open Veins of Latin America: Five Centuries of the Pillage of a Continent*, translated by Cedric Belfrage (London: Serpent's Tail, 2009).

Gobat, Michel, 'The Invention of Latin America: A Transnational History of Anti-Imperialism, Democracy, and Race', *American Historical Review*, vol. 118 no. 5 (December, 2013), pp. 1345–75.

The Golden Dream/La jaula de oro (dir. Diego Quemada-Díez, Mexico, 2013).

Klein, Naomi, *The Shock Doctrine: The Rise of Disaster Capitalism* (New York: Picador, 2008).

Mufwene, Salikoko S. (ed.), *Iberian Imperialism and Language Evolution in Latin America* (Chicago: University of Chicago Press, 2014); for Spanish and Maya in Yucatán see the chapter by Barbara Pfeiler.

Wollstonecraft, Mary, *A Vindication of the Rights of Woman*, revised edition (London: Penguin, 2004), pp. 141–2.

Index

www.ingramcontent.com/pod-product-compliance
Lightning Source LLC
LaVergne TN
LVHW010930110826
845149LV00013B/2535

9781350377035